D0846494

BRITAIN SAYS YES

The 1975 Referendum on
the Common Market

Anthony King

American Enterprise Institute for Public Policy Research
Washington, D.C.

ISBN 0-8447-3260-5

Library of Congress Catalog Card No. 77-83257

AEI Studies 160

Printed in the United States of America

CONTENTS

For to bear all naked truths
And to envisage circumstance, all calm,
That is the top of sovereignty.

Keats, *Hyperion*

PREFACE

A great deal of ink has already been spilt on the subject of Britain's 1975 Common Market referendum. In addition to the numerous books and articles arguing in general terms the pros and cons of holding national referenda in the United Kingdom, there already exist two substantial studies of the referendum: *The 1975 Referendum* by David Butler and Uwe Kitzinger, and Philip Goodhart's *Full-Hearted Consent*. Both of these books are well researched and are full of invaluable information. The present writer has drawn on them freely. How freely emerges from the footnotes to the pages that follow. If this book differs from the others, it is in two main respects. First, it is addressed to an American as well as to a British audience. Second, this book is concerned not so much with describing events as with trying to explain them—in large part, with trying to make sense of the actions of the chief protagonists.

The author is grateful for the help of a large number of people, in addition to the authors of the two studies just mentioned. Howard R. Penniman of the American Enterprise Institute first suggested that the present study be undertaken. John Bateman could not have been a more thorough or conscientious research assistant. Parts of the manuscript were read by David Robertson and Bo Särlvik. The whole of it was read, with great care and attention to detail, by Heather Bliss, Ivor Crewe, Jan Vergo, Peter Vergo, and Shirley Williams. I am grateful to all of them for the trouble they took, while of course absolving them of any responsibility for the errors of fact and interpretation that, despite their best efforts, the book still undoubtedly contains.

One personal word. I have tried in what follows to be accurate in my reporting of facts and fair in my judgments. But I have not hesitated to make judgments, about both people and events, and the reader is entitled to know where I stood on the Common Market issue. On June 5, 1975, I voted "yes." That seemed to me the right thing to do at the time. It still does.

ANTHONY KING

The Mill House
Wakes Colne, Essex
February 17, 1977

1
BRITAIN AND EUROPE
1945-1973

This short book seeks to explain why a referendum was held in June 1975 on whether or not Britain should remain a member of the European Community and why it resulted in an overwhelming majority in favor of Britain's staying in. The subject is of interest from several points of view. The political scientist will want to know how a country as conservative as Britain came to adopt a constitutional innovation as radical as the referendum. The student of public opinion will want to know why the British public, which for several years had seemed to be opposed to Britain's Common Market membership, in the end voted in favor of it. The student of European affairs will want to know what the referendum and its outcome reveal about the depth of Britain's commitment to European integration.[1]

The Labour party committed itself to holding a referendum or general election on the Common Market in the aftermath of its defeat in the June 1970 general election, and in many ways it would be convenient to begin our story at that point. But to understand why the Labour party committed itself in this way, and why British attitudes towards Europe evolved as they did, we need to go back a good deal further in time, to the years immediately following the Second World War.

In 1945 the economic and political leadership of Europe seemed on the face of it to be Britain's for the asking. Britain alone of the

---

[1] Here and throughout this book, the terms European Community, European Economic Community (EEC), and Common Market are used interchangeably. Pro-Europeans in Britain tended to use the phrase European Community, presumably because it sounded comforting and vaguely idealistic. Anti-Europeans preferred "Common Market," which sounded strictly commercial at the best of times and could be made to sound slightly sordid. But it did not matter which phrase was used; everyone knew what was meant.

1

major European powers had not been invaded or defeated. The prestige of its leaders and institutions was enormous. Its economy, though battered, was far stronger than that of its continental neighbors.[2] And at first Britain seemed willing to play a leadership role. Churchill had made his historic offer of joint Franco-British citizenship in 1940; in 1946, in a dramatic speech in Zurich, he called for the creation of a new "United States of Europe." Churchill was out of power by now, but the postwar Labour Government of Clement Attlee played a leading part in the Marshall Plan negotiations, in the setting up of the Brussels Treaty organization and later of NATO, and in creating the Council of Europe at Strasbourg.[3]

It gradually became clear, however, that Britain's ideas about the future of Europe differed fundamentally from those of its neighbors. They wanted to build a united Europe; Britain wanted to be "with" Europe but not "of" it.[4] When the Organization for European Economic Cooperation was set up in 1948 to administer American Marshall Plan aid, the British insisted that the new body should function strictly intergovernmentally and should not have autonomous decision-making powers of its own. In 1949 the British likewise blocked efforts to have a limited range of autonomous decision-making powers vested in the Committee of Ministers of the Council of Europe. The real breach came a year later, in 1950, when the Attlee Government refused to place Britain's coal and steel industries under a supranational authority. As a result, Britain did not take part in the Schuman Plan negotiations in the summer of 1950 and did not become a founder member of the new European Coal and Steel Community. The breach was widened by the Churchill ad-

---

[2] For example, British coal production was almost as large as that of all the rest of the countries that later formed the Organization for European Economic Cooperation combined. Crude steel production in Britain in 1947 was 12.7 million tons, while in the continental OEEC countries it was only 17.6 million tons, compared with 1938 figures of 10.6 and 34.9 million tons respectively. See Miriam Camps, *Britain and the European Community 1955-1963* (Princeton, N.J.: Princeton University Press, 1964), p. 3.

[3] The literature on the postwar history of Europe and on Britain's relations with the EEC is vast. This chapter is based largely on Camps, *Britain and the European Community*; Nora Beloff, *The General Says No: Britain's Exclusion from Europe* (Harmondsworth, Middlesex: Penguin Books, 1963); Uwe Kitzinger, *The Second Try: Labour and the EEC* (Oxford: Pergamon Press, 1968); Robert J. Lieber, *British Politics and European Unity: Parties, Elites, and Pressure Groups* (Berkeley, Calif.: University of California Press, 1970); Richard Mayne, *The Recovery of Europe: From Devastation to Unity* (London: Weidenfeld and Nicolson, 1970); and Roger Morgan, *West European Politics since 1945: The Shaping of the European Community* (London: B. T. Batsford, 1972).

[4] Lieber, *British Politics and European Unity*, p. 25.

ministration's refusal in 1952 to participate in the proposed European Defense Community, and was widened still further three years later, in 1955, when the Eden Government withdrew the sole British representative from the Spaak committee, which was working out the details of the European Economic Community and Euratom.

In later years, Britain's standoffishness in the forties and early fifties, its refusal to assist in building the new Europe, came to be regarded as a gross failure of statesmanship—a failure for which the British people were paying a heavy price. It is worth noting, therefore, what the causes of the failure were.

To begin with, it is important to recognize that there is no point in trying to place the blame on any one individual or on either of the political parties. No one was to blame, because everyone was. For example, when the Attlee Government announced in the spring of 1950 that Britain could not see its way to taking part in the Schuman Plan negotiations, it was attacked in the House of Commons by the Conservatives, who maintained that some way should have been found of associating Britain with the new developments. But in reality the Conservatives were at least as opposed as the Government to the creation of supranational institutions to which Britain would be subject. Ironically, in view of his later championing of the European cause, it was Harold Macmillan who put the point most forcefully in the debate:

> One thing is certain and we may as well face it. Our people are not going to hand to any supranational authority the right to close down our pits or steelworks. We will allow no supranational authority to put large masses of our people out of work in Durham, in the Midlands, in South Wales, or in Scotland.[5]

Even after the Conservatives were returned to power in 1951, they made no move to join the Coal and Steel Community, and, as we have seen, it was the Conservative Government of Sir Anthony Eden that kept Britain out of the EEC and Euratom. The Liberals began to press for Community membership in 1957, but neither of the two major parties took up the cause until the early 1960s.

The Conservative and Labour parties arrived at the same rather negative conclusions, but they arrived at them by different routes. In

---

[5] Quoted in Beloff, *The General Says No*, pp. 58-59. On the attitude of the Conservatives in the early 1950s, see Mayne, *Recovery of Europe*, Chapters 8 and 9; Harold Macmillan, *Tides of Fortune 1945-1955* (London: Macmillan, 1969), Chapter 8; and Margaret Laing, *Edward Heath, Prime Minister* (London: Sidgwick & Jackson, 1972), pp. 95-98.

view of later events, it is interesting to note that there can be detected on the Labour side from a very early stage the feeling that the continental countries were somehow inherently "capitalist" in a way that Britain was not. The Labour Government in the years just after the war was engaged in "building socialism"—not only in expanding the scope of the welfare state but in taking key sectors of the economy into public ownership. The Labour party had waited for forty years to come to power and was not prepared to brook interference from outside. But, while Britain was moving to the left, the Continent was moving to the right. In Italy, the Communists and Socialists left the government in 1947; in France, after the fall of *tripartisme* in the same year, successive governments were increasingly dominated by center and center-right coalitions; in Germany, politics was dominated by the rise of the conservative Adenauer. The economies of almost all of the continental countries seemed to be reverting to their prewar pattern. It is therefore hardly surprising that the Labour party declared in 1950:

> No Socialist Party with the prospect of forming a government could accept a system by which important fields of national policy were surrendered to a supra-national European representative authority, since such an authority would have a permanently anti-Socialist majority. . . . The Labour Party could never accept any commitments which limited its own or others' freedom to pursue democratic socialism. . . .[6]

Had the postwar Labour Government felt any strong desire to forge close links with Europe, these considerations would undoubtedly have constituted an obstacle. They might—who knows?—have constituted an insurmountable obstacle. But the postwar Labour Government did not in fact have any such desire; nor did the Conservative Governments that came after it. The main reasons why Britain stood aloof from Europe were common to the two major political parties and were not primarily ideological in character.

The British governments after 1945 were preoccupied governments. Although Britain emerged from the war stronger economically than most of its neighbors, its position was still highly precarious— far more precarious than was generally realized. The larger part of its foreign investments had been liquidated during the war, and Britain had to export on a massive scale to pay for essential imports of food and raw materials. The success of this "export drive" was

---

[6] Kitzinger, *The Second Try*, pp. 69, 61.

outstanding—between 1946 and 1950 the value of British exports increased by 77 percent in real terms—but Britain's balance of payments remained in chronic deficit, and government ministers feared that at any moment there might have to be a drastic cut in the people's standard of living.[7] A former senior civil servant has recalled how, when he joined the Treasury in 1947, one of his first tasks was to devise plans in case the foreign reserves ran out. The experts had calculated that the food ration would then drop to 1,800 calories per day, against 2,700 at the worst moment of the war.[8] At the same time as it was grappling with the country's economic problems, the Labour Government was engaged in its task of social reconstruction, was heavily preoccupied together with the United States in meeting the challenge of the Soviet Union, and was working out how best to grant independence to the nations of the Indian subcontinent. British ministers and the British government machine were both working at full stretch after 1945. Talk of "building Europe" was merely an unwelcome distraction.

The scale of Britain's problems might, of course, have drawn Britain closer to the Continent if British politicians had believed that the continental countries had anything to contribute to solving them. But they did not. Most of the countries on the Continent were even worse off than Britain; they constituted neither sources of raw materials for Britain nor markets for British exports. Britain indeed was having to pump substantial amounts of economic aid into its zone of occupied Germany. The other European countries could not contribute substantially until about 1950 to the containment of the U.S.S.R., and they had little to say to Britain's problems of decolonization; on the contrary, whereas Britain after 1945 was trying to shed its empire in Asia, the French were preparing to fight to retain theirs in Indochina. Not only did the continentals' talk of "building Europe" not seem to have anything to offer Britain; almost no one in Britain believed that much would come of it. The dream of the Continent was a united Europe; the reality was economic chaos and unstable minority governments. The dream seemed simply a way of escaping from the reality. It was—but in a different sense from what the British supposed.

On top of all this, Britain in the immediate postwar years was still, or at least believed itself to be, a world power. Britain alone, apart from the United States and the U.S.S.R., possessed the atomic

---

[7] See Sidney Pollard, *The Development of the British Economy 1914-1967* (London: Edward Arnold, 1969), chapter 7.

[8] Quoted in Beloff, *The General Says No*, p. 51.

bomb; Britain alone, apart from them, was developing the hydrogen bomb. The British Empire, though much diminished by the loss of India and Burma, was still one of the greatest empires the world had ever known and seemed likely to endure into the 1980s and 1990s—conceivably into the next century. British soldiers served in the ten years after 1945 in Korea (Britain alone of the European powers sent troops to Korea), in the jungles of Malaya, along the Suez Canal, and on the slopes of Mount Kilimanjaro. Whereas the horizons of the continental countries, even including France, were already largely bounded by the frontiers of Europe, Britain's seemed to have no limit. Successive British Governments conceived of Britain as forming part of three great circles, the first linking Britain with the United States, the second linking it with the British Commonwealth and Empire, the third linking it with Europe. For many years after 1945 the European circle seemed, both economically and militarily, the least important of the three.[9]

Its preoccupations, its national interests, and its self-image thus combined to keep Britain apart from Europe. But there were other factors, more subtle than the others and if anything even more pervasive: Englishmen and Scotsmen simply did not think like Europeans and did not think of themselves as Europeans. To the purely political sources of division were added psychological factors. Again, it was left to Harold Macmillan to draw attention to one of the most important, in a speech at Strasbourg in 1950:

> The difference is temperamental and intellectual. It is based on a long divergence of two states of mind and methods of argumentation. The continental tradition likes to reason *a priori* from the top downwards, from the general principles to the practical application. It is the tradition of St. Thomas Aquinas, of the schoolmen, and of the great continental scholars and thinkers. The Anglo-Saxons like to argue *a posteriori* from the bottom upwards, from practical experience. It is the tradition of Bacon and Newton.[10]

More immediately, it was hard for the British, who had emerged from the war a united people, victorious and confident, to appreciate fully the psychological ravages that the war had wrought on the Continent and to absorb the fact that, for the French, the Germans, and the Italians, the building of a united Europe was not a vague aspiration but a political imperative. The British were not conscious

---

[9] See Lieber, *British Politics and European Unity*, pp. 17-18. Churchill in particular was much wedded to the three-circles concept.
[10] Quoted in Beloff, *The General Says No*, p. 60.

6

of any such necessity. The countries of Europe were "over there," foreign, alien. The mentality that produced the newspaper headline "Fog Isolates Continent" survived. Sir Anthony Eden was probably speaking for the vast majority of his fellow countrymen when he told an American audience in 1952 that joining a European federation was "something which we know, in our bones, we cannot do."[11]

For all of these reasons, Britain did not join the European Coal and Steel Community in 1950 and did not sign the Treaty of Rome in 1957. In one sense, the British chose not to participate in building a united Europe; they could have taken part in the various negotiations and signed the various treaties but did not. But, in another sense, they did not choose. To choose is to consider various alternatives and to select from among them. British governments after 1945 never really seriously considered the European alternative. To have done so would have required a spectacular leap of political imagination. Britain's leaders after 1945 were not so imaginative. It is doubtful whether the leaders of any other country, similarly placed, would have been either.

Beginning in about 1958, however, Britain's circumstances, and politicians' perceptions of them, began to change. Although the late 1950s were years of unparalleled material prosperity in Britain—the Conservative party won the 1959 general election on the slogan "Life's better under the Conservatives: don't let Labour ruin it"—the problems of managing the British economy came to seem more and more intractable as the decade wore on. A period of rapid economic growth would invariably be followed by a balance-of-payments crisis, as the rise in British exports failed to keep pace with the rise in imports. In order to overcome the crisis, the government would take steps to reduce domestic demand, whereupon industrial investment would fall and unemployment gradually rise. At some point, investment would have fallen too far, or unemployment risen too high, or the balance-of-payments position would have righted itself, whereupon the government would take steps to reflate demand. There would then follow a brief period of rapid economic growth, which

---

[11] Morgan, *West European Politics*, p. 135. In the late 1940s Sir Stafford Cripps, the Labour chancellor of the exchequer, was having lunch with Averell Harriman, the American administrator of Marshall Plan aid. Cripps was irked by Harriman's continuous prodding over Britain's reluctance to go into Europe and asked Harriman how he would feel if the United Kingdom kept asking the United States to get into bed with Brazil. Harriman admitted that he would not like it. "Well," Sir Stafford said, "that's how we feel about France." (Beloff, *The General Says No*, p. 53). See also Camps, *Britain and the European Community*, p. 3, and Uwe Kitzinger, *The Challenge of the Common Market* (Oxford: Basil Blackwell, 1961), p. 3.

would invariably be followed by a balance-of-payments crisis, which would invariably be followed in turn by government steps to reduce demand. . . . And so it went.

The "stop-go" cycle, as it came to be called, was discouraging in itself; it suggested that the Keynesian techniques of economic management were no longer working. More important, by undermining business confidence, it appeared to be a major explanation of Britain's poor overall economic performance. Britain's economy in the late 1950s was growing all right, but very, very slowly. Between 1953 and 1958, the British gross national product rose in real terms at an average annual rate of 2.2 percent. During the same period, France's growth rate averaged 4.6 percent, Italy's 5.2 percent and West Germany's a phenomenal 6.9 percent. The rate of growth for all six countries that made up the European Economic Community was 5.3 percent—more than double that of Britain. Between 1958 and 1964, Britain's rate of growth was to increase quite substantially, to 3.9 percent, but the countries of the Six continued to grow even faster; their growth rate in the same years was 5.6 percent.[12] The balance of economic power had swung decisively against Britain since the years immediately after the war.

Against this background, it was hardly surprising that the European Community—only three years old by 1960 but already well established—loomed larger and larger in the calculations of British policy makers. The Community constituted a threat; it also held out a promise. On the one hand, unless Britain could come to some satisfactory agreement with the EEC, there was the danger that British firms would find it increasingly difficult to compete in continental markets. On the other, the Community offered British manufacturers a market of 180 million persons—even larger than that of the United States. It offered them a chance to take advantage of economies of scale; it offered them the challenge, which many of them were eager to accept, of increased competition. At first the British government sought to make a deal with the EEC without actually joining it; there was much talk of creating an industrial free trade area and of "building bridges" between EEC members and nonmemebrs. But the Six were not interested in such arrangements, and it gradually became clear that the choice for Britain was the straightforward one of joining the EEC or not.

These economic considerations were reinforced by political factors. Indeed in the minds of many British policy makers the

---

[12] OECD figures quoted in Uwe Kitzinger, *The European Common Market and Community* (London: Routledge & Kegan Paul, 1967), p. 74.

political factors were the more important. By the early 1960s, it was clear that two of the three great circles that formed the basis of British foreign policy—the "special relationship" with the United States, and the British Commonwealth and Empire—were fast disintegrating, or at least were radically changing their shape. The Americans had long favored moves towards European unity; they inevitably took the countries of the Continent more and more seriously as these countries grew in economic strength; and, equally inevitably, they became impatient with British standoffishness. The Kennedy administration, beginning in 1961, sought to create an "Atlantic partnership" between the United States and a united Western Europe. Kennedy and his closest advisers tended to be anglophiles, but they perceived clearly the extent of Britain's decline in the world and were conscious that, if Britain remained outside Europe, America's diplomatic tasks in Europe would be much harder to fulfill. When Macmillan, by now British prime minister, visited Kennedy in Washington in April 1961, he was surprised to discover that the American president, far from being unhappy at the idea that Britain might join the Common Market, was enthusiastically in favor.[13]

Behind Britain's growing isolation in the world lay the transformation of the British Commonwealth. The British were quickly reconciled to the loss of their empire after 1945, but they were reconciled to it partly because they believed that their leadership of the Commonwealth would enable them to continue to play a world role. They also believed that the poorer nations of the Commonwealth would continue to be major suppliers of British foodstuffs and raw materials and major markets for British exports. But by about 1969 it was dawning on British policy makers, and on Conservative members of Parliament, that the new-style Commonwealth was not amenable to British political leadership, that its character was being changed fundamentally by the accession of new Asian and African member states, and that British trade with the Commonwealth was tending to stagnate while British trade with Europe and the rest of the developed world was expanding rapidly. For many Conservative M.P.s the moment of truth came in April 1961 when South Africa, Britain's ally in two world wars, was in effect expelled from the Commonwealth by a coalition of the newer members.[14] Forced in earlier years to choose between Europe and the Commonwealth,

---

[13] See Camps, *Britain and the European Community*, pp. 336-37.

[14] The coalition was led, rather surprisingly, by Canada. It is clear, however, that if the old members of the Commonwealth had been left to their own devices South Africa would have remained inside.

many in Britain, especially in the Conservative party, would have found the choice difficult; but from 1960–1961 onwards the choice was no longer there. It was Europe or nothing.

The shift in British opinion towards Europe, when it finally did come, came astonishingly quickly. A young Treasury official, long a convinced advocate of Britain's entry into the EEC, later recalled that, whereas in 1959 the very idea was enough to cause him to be dismissed as a long-haired eccentric, in 1960 it was becoming reasonably acceptable, and by 1961 to be opposed to it was to be regarded as a stick-in-the-mud.[15] Inside Whitehall, the lead was taken by Sir Frank Lee, a senior official who became permanent secretary to the Treasury at the beginning of 1960.[16] Outside, although the Federation of British Industry as an organization was inclined to be negative, more and more large industrial firms came round to the view that entry was essential, and the view of the press was also increasingly favorable. The *Guardian* probably spoke for a majority of informed opinion in Britain when it wrote on May 27, 1960, "the choice is between swimming in the main stream and vegetating in a backwater."[17]

We will probably never know exactly when Macmillan made up his own mind in favor of entry. Perhaps he does not even know himself. Certainly his memoirs are uninformative on the subject.[18] But it is clear that all of the considerations that weighed with others weighed with him, and he was especially sensitive to the decline in Britain's capacity to exert independent influence in the world. He was badly shaken by the cancellation of the Blue Streak rocket program in April 1960—Blue Streak represented Britain's last effort to remain self-sufficient in the field of nuclear armaments—and even more by the collapse in the following month of the summit conference in Paris, which he had done so much to bring about.

---

[15] Beloff, *The General Says No*, p. 89.

[16] On the crucial role played by Sir Frank Lee, see Camps, *Britain and the European Community*, pp. 280-81; Beloff, *The General Says No*, pp. 88-90; and Samuel Brittan, *Steering the Economy*, rev. ed. (Harmondsworth, Middlesex: Penguin Books, 1971), p. 237. The case of Lee well illustrates the importance of civil servants in the making of public policy in Britain.

[17] Camps, *Britain and the European Community*, p. 288. On the evolution of business attitudes, see Lieber, *British Politics and European Unity*, pp. 92-98, and Stephen Blank, *Government and Industry in Britain: The Federation of British Industry in Politics, 1945-65* (Westmead, Farnborough, Hampshire: Saxon House, Lexington Books, 1973), chapter 5.

[18] Harold Macmillan, *At the End of the Day, 1961-1963* (London: Macmillan, 1973), chapters 1, 5. The six volumes of Macmillan's memoirs must say less at greater length than any other set of memoirs in existence.

Not only was Britain's position in the world becoming increasingly lonely; the world, it seemed, was becoming more hostile. Whenever the Government's final decision was taken, British pronouncements on Europe grew sensibly warmer from the summer of 1960 onwards. In November 1960 Macmillan called for European economic unity in a speech to the United Kingdom Council of the European Movement. In the following February Edward Heath, the minister in charge of European negotiations at the Foreign Office, announced that the United Kingdom was prepared to accept the Community's common external tariff in principle. In April Macmillan had his crucial meeting in Washington with Kennedy. In June senior British cabinet ministers visited Commonwealth capitals to sound out Commonwealth opinion on the Common Market. And finally, on July 31, 1961, the prime minister announced in the House of Commons that Britain was applying for full EEC membership. It was just over ten years since Britain had refused to join the Coal and Steel Community.

In the end, the first British attempt to join the EEC proved abortive. After nearly eighteen months of negotiations between Britain and the EEC, President de Gaulle of France vetoed Britain's application on January 14, 1963. He feared that British membership would diminish the dominant role of France in the Community; more important, he was profoundly suspicious of Britain's close links with the United States. But, although de Gaulle's attitude kept Britain out of the Community for the time being, the considerations that had finally drawn Britain towards Europe lost none of their force as time passed. On the contrary, the arguments in favor of British membership of the EEC came in time to seem more, not less, powerful.

The Conservatives, after thirteen long years in office, were defeated in the general election of 1964. Harold Wilson's new Labour administration did not at once raise the European issue. On the one hand, de Gaulle's veto was still in force. On the other, Labour's attitude towards Europe, as we have already seen, was one of some suspicion. When the Conservatives applied for admission in 1961, Labour at first took up a position of studied neutrality; in August 1961 the Labour opposition in the House of Commons did not vote against the Conservative Government's pro-Common Market motion. But gradually, between the summer of 1961 and the autumn of 1962, the party's position hardened into one of outright hostility. At Labour's annual conference in October 1962, the party leader, Hugh Gaitskell, spoke of "the end of a thousand years of history" and set out conditions for British membership of the EEC which he must have

11

known could never be met.[19] Gaitskell's views were endorsed by Wilson, who succeeded him as party leader only four months later, and it is all but certain that, if de Gaulle had not imposed his veto and if the Brussels negotiations had been successful, the majority of the Labour party would have campaigned vigorously against British entry in 1963.

But, just as the Conservatives had been educated by the hard experience of trying to govern Britain from outside the Community, so now Labour's leaders learned that Britain's room for maneuver in the world was much smaller than they had supposed. The main difference was that, whereas the Conservatives' conversion took some five years, Labour's took not much more than eighteen months. Already, by the time of the second general election in March 1966, a number of senior Labour ministers were indicating in their speeches that they regarded British membership of the Common Market as desirable, even inevitable.[20]

Before they came to power, almost everyone on the Labour side imagined that, if the country was having a hard time of it under the Conservatives, as indeed it was, it was the Conservatives' fault. If only Labour were the government, the economy would grow faster, "stop-go" would no longer be necessary, the balance-of-payments position would be put right, new links would be forged with the Commonwealth, and Britain would again enjoy that place in the sun to which its past glories entitled it. "The Labour Party," said the party's manifesto in 1964, "is offering Britain a new way of life that will stir our hearts, re-kindle an authentic patriotic faith in our future, and enable our country to re-establish itself as a stable force in the world today for progress, peace, and justice."[21]

But somehow things did not work out quite like that. The new Labour Government suffered grave disappointments, economic and political. Economically, the problems both of growth and of the balance of payments proved intractable, at least in the short term. In 1965, the first full year of Labour government, Britain's gross

---

[19] *Report of the Sixty-First Annual Conference of the Labour Party*, Brighton, 1962 (London: Labour party, 1962), pp. 154-65.

[20] George Brown, then the minister for economic affairs, for example, insisted that Europe was not an issue between the parties and that the question was not whether Britain would join the EEC but when. See Lieber, *British Politics and European Unity*, pp. 244-45.

[21] *Let's Go with Labour for the New Britain*, the Labour party's manifesto for the 1964 general election, in F.W.S. Craig, ed., *British General Election Manifestos 1918-1966* (Chichester, Sussex: Political Reference Publications, 1970), p. 246.

national product rose by 2.4 percent; but West Germany's rose by 5.2 percent and the rate of growth for the Community as a whole was 4.1 percent, nearly double that of Britain. In 1966, Britain's growth rate fell back, to 1.4 percent. The Community's growth rate also fell back, to 3.9 percent; but, even so, the Community's rate of growth was more than double Britain's, and no EEC country had a growth rate of under 2.4 percent.[22] In other words, the gap between Britain and the European Community, already wide, was growing wider. Moreover, Labour in 1964 had declared that it would mobilize the nation's resources in a new "national plan."[23] But by 1966 the economic premises upon which the national plan was based had turned out to be false, and the plan itself was abandoned. Worst of all, the new Government found that it could not get the better of the balance-of-payments problem. Labour had inherited from the Conservatives a balance-of-payments deficit, on current and capital account, of £776 million. The deficit fell somewhat in the next two years, but, despite the imposition of a surcharge on imports and restrictions on capital outflows, the deficit was still £342 million in 1965 and £133 million in 1966. In 1966 it was already clear that the balance-of-payments position would worsen in 1967; in the end, the deficit that year was £540 million.[24] As a result, the story of the years 1964–1967 was in large part the story of Labour's desperate attempts —in the end unavailing—to avoid having to devalue the pound.

Politically, the problems confronting the new Government were less acute but, if anything, even more unsettling. Labour's 1964 manifesto devoted as much space to foreign and defense policy as to the economy—much more than to the social services. Britain under the Tories, the manifesto declared, had been "forced to linger temporarily in the wings of history."[25] The implication was that Britain under Labour would again become a world power. The manifesto laid particular stress on the importance for Britain of the Common-

---

[22] The figures are quoted in Kitzinger, The Second Try, p. 327.

[23] The New Britain in Craig, General Election Manifestos, p. 233. It would be difficult to exaggerate either Labour's optimism about indicative economic planning or the disarray into which the failure of planning threw the party's economic thinking. On the failure of the National Plan, see Samuel Brittan, Inquest on Planning in Britain (London: Political and Economic Planning, 1967); Jack Hayward and Michael Watson, eds., Planning, Politics and Public Policy: The British, French and Italian Experience (Cambridge: Cambridge University Press, 1975), chapters 2 and 5; and C.T. Sandford, National Economic Planning (London: Heinemann, 1972), chapters 4-5.

[24] British Central Statistical Office figures quoted in Kitzinger, The Second Try, p. 336.

[25] The New Britain in Craig, General Election Manifestos, p. 241.

wealth. "Though," it said, "we shall seek to achieve closer links with our European neighbours, the Labour Party is convinced that the first responsibility of a British Government is still to the Common-wealth."[26] From this point of view, Labour's first eighteen months in office were deeply disillusioning. The new Commonwealth nations refused to help the Government control the influx of Common-wealth immigrants into Britain and were vociferously critical of Britain's failure to use force against the white settlers in Rhodesia. Indeed the Rhodesian episode was doubly humiliating: Wilson and his colleagues found that they could not prevent the white Rho-desians from declaring their independence unilaterally, and then found that they were powerless to impose effective economic sanctions to bring Rhodesia to heel. As for the special relationship with the United States, it soon emerged that, although the usual politenesses would be exchanged, the United States did not regard the United Kingdom as a more important ally than, say, France or West Germany and, in the absence of British troops, was not disposed to take very seriously the Wilson Government's numerous efforts to mediate in the war in Vietnam. Britain's prime minister was welcome in Wash-ington, to be sure, but then so were many other foreign statesmen.

The essential discovery made by Labour was the same as that made already by the Conservatives: that Britain's power to shape its own destiny, much less other people's, was strictly limited, and that Kennedy's famous 1962 "declaration of interdependence" had been in fact not so much a pious assertion of hopes for the future as a bald statement of present international realities.[27] James Callaghan, Labour's chancellor of the exchequer, put the point well in a speech in the House of Commons soon after Britain again applied for EEC membership:

> My experience over the last two and a half years has led me to the conclusion more and more that to a very large extent nations are not free at the moment to make their own decisions. This is becoming increasingly true, as I have observed in financial, economic and political matters, and is certainly not limited to the United Kingdom. . . . I have been struck by the effect of the international forums in the world today on the policies of individual countries,

---

[26] Ibid. p. 242.
[27] Extracts from Kennedy's declaration can be found in Kitzinger, *European Common Market and Community*, pp. 165-68.

an effect which is much more than I had assumed before I took office. . . . The argument about sovereignty is rapidly becoming outdated.[28]

During the March 1966 election campaign, although some ministers made pro-European noises, the prime minister reserved his position. He indicated that, other things being equal, he would like Britain to join the Common Market, but his general tone was not pro-European and he continued to lay down stringent conditions. It seems probable, however, that he had already decided that Britain's future lay in Europe, and the Queen's Speech at the opening of the new Parliament mentioned Britain's readiness to join the EEC provided that its conditions—unspecified—could be met. In November Wilson announced in the House of Commons that he and his colleagues were about to embark on bilateral discussions with the heads of government of the Six to find out whether essential British interests could be safeguarded if Britain adhered to the Rome Treaty. The discussions took place during the early months of 1967, and on May 2, 1967, the prime minister reported to Parliament that the Government had decided to apply formally for EEC membership.[29]

Britain in 1967 was drawn towards Europe for much the same reasons as in 1961; Britain apart from Europe appeared doomed to economic stagnation and political isolation. But the balance of the argument had shifted slightly, in two significant respects. In the first place, the economic argument had been broadened. In the early sixties the Conservative Government's aim had been the straightforward one of ensuring that British exporters could compete on an equal basis in continental markets. By 1967 politicians and industrialists throughout Europe had become aware that high-technology industries like aviation, computers, and atomic energy were going to depend for their future on the availability of large markets and also on enormous injections of government funds for research and development. No single country anywhere offered a market on the requisite scale; no single European government could afford to foot the research-and-development bill for more than one or two major projects. If high technology were not to become an American monopoly, the countries of Europe would have to work more closely together. The force of this argument was felt fully as much in Britain

---

[28] Quoted in Kitzinger, *The Second Try*, p. 4.
[29] On the Labour Government's 1967 application, see Kitzinger, *The Second Try*; Miriam Camps, *European Unification in the Sixties: From the Veto to the Crisis* (New York: McGraw-Hill, 1966), chapter 5; Mayne, *Recovery of Europe*, chapter 11; and Lieber, *British Politics and European Unity*, chapter 9.

as on the Continent—if anything, even more so since Britain was the European leader in many advanced-technology fields.[30]

In the second place, Wilson and his colleagues were much readier to admit in 1967 than the Conservatives had been six years earlier that, important as the economic argument was, it was the political argument that was on balance decisive. On the economic side, there were, after all, costs to be incurred as well as benefits to be gained; if Britain joined the EEC, its imports of food were certain to be more costly in the future, and no one denied that, at least at first, EEC membership would place a heavy, perhaps an insupportable, burden on the balance of payments. But on the political side, while the costs of membership seemed likely to be negligible, the benefits were bound to be great. With the Commonwealth in disarray and the Johnson administration in the United States increasingly preoccupied with Southeast Asia at Europe's expense, Britain could only gain by being more closely associated with the other European powers. There was no longer anything at all splendid about splendid isolation. Recognition of this fact was much more widespread in Britain in 1967 than it had been in Macmillan's time, and it was easier for the Labour Government than it would have been for the Conservatives to state openly that Britain was seeking to join not just a customs union but a body whose ultimate aim was European political union.[31]

But again, in 1967 as in 1963, Britain's application ran onto the rocks of Gaullist opposition. On May 16, 1967, only a fortnight after Wilson's announcement that Britain intended to apply for membership again, de Gaulle at his press conference rehearsed at length the obstacles to British membership and indicated that, before seeking to join, Britain should undergo a fundamental economic and political transformation. Wilson responded the next day, saying that Britain did not intend to take no for an answer; but no the answer was to be. Although the European Commission endorsed the British application in October 1967, on November 27, de Gaulle roundly declared that British membership would be incompatible with the continued existence of the Community in its present form. It was clear, as it had been in 1963, that, if the British persisted with their application, the French would ultimately veto it—as they and every other Community member had the power to do under the Rome treaty.

In the short term, then, the prospects for British membership of

---

[30] See Camps, *European Unification in the Sixties*, pp. 158-59, and Mayne, *Recovery of Europe*, pp. 277-78.

[31] See Camps, *European Unification in the Sixties*, pp. 159-61.

the EEC looked bleak. But in the long term, and even in the medium term, they looked much brighter. In Britain, a Labour Government was now committed to seeking entry, and the Conservative party was, if anything, even more pro-European now than it had been under Macmillan. The party's new leader, Edward Heath, had made his maiden speech in the House of Commons on the theme of European unity, had led the British side in the Brussels negotiations in 1961–1963 and had fought the 1966 election campaign largely on the European issue. His commitment to a united Europe was total. On the Continent, the only Community member that did not want Britain to join was France and increasingly France's opposition was personal to de Gaulle. Most other French politicians, even among the Gaullists, either were not opposed to British entry or, even though opposed, believed that on balance France was paying too high a price for its opposition in terms of its relations with the other members of the Six. By the late 1960s, it was generally believed both on the Continent and in Britain that, although much hard bargaining lay ahead, British membership of the Community was virtually certain once President de Gaulle was gone.

De Gaulle finally disappeared from the scene in 1969. He resigned in April after being defeated in a referendum on a domestic political matter and he died in the following year. His successor, Georges Pompidou, indicated shortly after his election that he was not in principle opposed to Britain's joining the EEC, and at a Community summit conference in December 1969 it was agreed that if possible the Community should be enlarged. Later the date of June 30, 1970, was set for the opening of negotiations between the Six and the four countries applying for membership—Ireland, Norway, and Denmark as well as the United Kingdom.

In Britain, a general election, on June 18, intervened. Labour's manifesto for the election, while emphasizing that British and Commonwealth interests needed to be safeguarded, asserted that the forthcoming negotiations would be "pressed with determination."[32] The Conservatives' likewise, though with rather more qualifications, declared that membership in the European Community would "make a major contribution to both the prosperity and the security of our country."[33] The Conservatives' surprise victory in the election did not prevent the negotiations from opening, on schedule, in Luxem-

---

[32] *Now Britain's strong let's make it great to live in,* the Labour party's manifesto for the 1970 general election (London: Labour party, 1970), p. 28.

[33] *A Better Tomorrow,* the Conservative party's manifesto for the 1970 general election (London: Conservative Central Office, 1970), p. 28.

bourg on June 30, 1970. Twelve months later, in June 1971, agreement on all the main issues between Britain and the Six had been reached, and in October 1971 the House of Commons voted to accept the Government's terms. The Treaty of Accession was signed in Brussels in January 1972; the necessary enabling legislation, the European Communities Act, passed through both houses of Parliament during the course of 1972; and on January 1, 1973, Britain became a full member of the European Community. For Edward Heath the successful outcome of the negotiations was a personal triumph. "For twenty-five years," he told the British people, "we have been looking for something to get us going again. Now here it is."[34]

In the normal course of events, our story, and this book, would have ended at this point. British membership in the EEC would have been an accomplished fact. But the course of events was not normal between 1970 and 1973, and it was not to be normal again for another two-and-a-half years. For in the weeks and months after its loss of office in June 1970 the Labour party, having in office been firmly committed in favor of British EEC membership, swung around in opposition to the point where it was all but committed to opposing it. By 1973 the party had pledged itself to renegotiate the Conservative Government's terms of entry and to put the whole issue of Britain's membership in the EEC to the British people, by means of either a general election or a referendum. In Chapters 3 and 4 we shall consider why Labour's views about Europe changed and how the party came to adopt the principle of holding a national referendum. Before we do, however, we need to pause briefly to consider the state of public opinion in Britain with regard to Europe during the period we have already dealt with, and also to consider the relationship between public opinion and the policy making of successive British governments. As we shall see, the state of public opinion in the 1960s will explain much that was to happen in the 1970s.

---

[34] See Anthony King, "The Election that Everyone Lost" in Howard R. Penniman, ed., *Britain at the Polls: The Parliamentary Elections of 1974* (Washington, D.C.: American Enterprise Institute, 1975), p. 8. A full account of the negotiations leading up to Britain's accession to the Treaty of Rome can be found in Uwe Kitzinger, *Diplomacy and Persuasion: How Britain Joined the Common Market* (London: Thames and Hudson, 1973), chapters 1-5.

2
THE STATE OF PUBLIC OPINION
1961-1973

The preceding chapter focused on successive governments and, to a much lesser extent, on business and civil service opinion and the press—without taking into account the state of public opinion. We reported on the actions of successive governments; we did not report on how far these governments, in acting as they did, were responding to the preferences of the mass electorate.

This omission is easily explained. British policy towards Europe in the 1960s and early 1970s was made almost entirely at the elite level. British governments did not act in response to popular demands; neither were they constrained in any serious way by the fear that their policies might bring retribution at the polls. To be sure, politicians of all parties included Europe somewhere in their electoral calculations. Harold Macmillan in 1961 hoped that his bid to enter Europe would give the Tory party a new look after more than a decade in office.[1] Similarly, Harold Wilson during the election campaign of 1966, detecting some popular uneasiness about Europe, attacked the Conservatives for not being concerned enough to safeguard British interests.[2] But most British politicians between 1961 and 1973 seem to have sensed, however dimly, that the European issue was not going to sway many votes one way or the other. If this was their view, they were almost certainly correct.

Table 2-1 is based on Gallup poll data. It shows how British

---

[1] See Beloff, The General Says No, pp. 95-96, and D. E. Butler and Anthony King, The British General Election of 1964 (London: Macmillan, 1965), pp. 78-80.

[2] Wilson maintained that the Labour Government would negotiate its way into Europe, not crawl. He contrasted his own position with that of Heath: "Now one encouraging gesture from the French Government, which I welcome, and the Conservative leader rolls on his back like a spaniel. . . . Some of my best friends are spaniels, but I would not put them in charge of negotiations into the Common Market." Quoted in Lieber, British Politics and European Unity, p. 245.

Table 2-1
RESPONSES TO QUESTIONS, VARIOUSLY WORDED, ABOUT WHETHER OR NOT BRITAIN SHOULD JOIN THE COMMON MARKET
(in percentages)

Q: If the British Government were to decide that Britain's interest would best be served by joining the European Common Market, would you approve or disapprove?

	Approve	Disapprove	Don't Know
July 1960	49	13	38
July 1961	44	20	36
July 1962	42	25	33
January 1963	41	30	29
July 1965	56	22	22
June 1966	61	16	23
March 1967	57	27	16

Q: Do you approve or disapprove of the Government applying for membership of the Common Market?

	Approve	Disapprove	Don't Know
June 1967	40	45	15
July 1968	36	43	21
November 1969	36	45	19
April 1970	19	59	22
August 1970	21	56	23
May 1971	23	59	18

Q: On the facts as you know them at present are you for or against Britain joining the Common Market?

	For	Against	Don't Know
August 1971	36	47	17
May 1972	41	45	14
August 1972	40	42	18

Q: Do you think that we were right or wrong to join the Common Market?

	Right	Wrong	Don't Know
January 1973	38	36	26
June 1973	39	44	17
November 1973	34	48	18

Source: *Gallup Political Index.*

public opinion towards the Common Market evolved between 1960, when the possibility of British entry first began to be discussed seriously, and late 1973, shortly after Britain had become an EEC member. The table needs to be interpreted with some caution since the question asked by Gallup on the Common Market was changed in 1965 and again in 1971; but the general picture that emerges is clear enough.[3] Between 1960 and 1966 the balance of public opinion was in favor of Britain's joining Europe. From 1967 onwards, except for a brief period early in 1973, it was broadly against. One might be inclined to infer that Europe was a potential vote-winner before 1967, a potential vote-loser thereafter. The truth, however, is a good deal more complicated.

What does it mean to say of someone that he has an "opinion" on an issue? At one extreme, it may mean very little. It may mean only that the individual in question, if asked for his view in an opinion survey, will offer a response; he will answer "yes" or "no" to a straight yes-no question. But he may be responding simply because he has been asked to respond. He may know little about the issue, may not have thought about it, and may not have any feelings about it. Indeed he may respond more or less at random, answering "yes" to the question at one moment, "no" at the next. Having an opinion in this sense amounts to little more than not wanting to admit to the interviewer that one actually does not have an opinion. Yet, in the tables reporting the findings of opinion surveys, these "opinions" are indistinguishable from all other kinds of opinions; seemingly stable overall patterns of public opinion may conceal large numbers of self-cancelling shifts of "opinion" in this sense.[4]

[3]Moreover, all of the other polls agreed that this was the picture. The main series are to be found in the Gallup Poll's monthly *Gallup Political Index* and in National Opinion Polls' monthly *NOP Political Bulletin*. Among the many other sources of opinion poll data on Europe are B. Hedges and R. Jowell, *Britain and the EEC: Report on a Survey of Attitudes towards the European Economic Community* (London: Social and Community Planning Research, 1971); Robert J. Shepherd, *Public Opinion and European Integration* (Westmead, Farnborough, Hampshire: Saxon House, Lexington Books, 1975); Roger Jowell and James Spence, *The Grudging Europeans: A Study of British Attitudes towards the ECC* (London: Social and Community Planning Research, 1975); and Frank Teer and James D. Spence, *Political Opinion Polls* (London: Hutchinson, 1973), pp. 108-20. It should be said that in their subsidiary findings, as well as in their main ones, the various polling organizations produced results that were remarkably similar—both in the 1961-1973 period and later.

[4] On the phenomenon of "response uncertainty," see Philip Converse, "The Nature of Belief Systems in Mass Publics" in D. E. Apter, ed., *Ideology and Discontent* (New York: Free Press of Glencoe, 1964), pp. 206-61, and David Butler and Donald Stokes, *Political Change in Britain: The Evolution of Electoral Choice*, 2d ed. (London: Macmillan, 1974), chapters 13 and 14.

At the other extreme, to say that someone has an opinion on an issue may be to say much more. It may be to say that the person in question knows something about the issue, has thought about it, and probably has reasonably strong feelings about it. A person who holds an opinion in this sense can usually give reasons for holding the opinion he does, and he is unlikely very often to change his mind. He may change it—of course. But he is likely to change it only in response to some important alteration either in the outside world or in his own outlook on life. It was "opinion" of this kind—well-formed opinion, if not necessarily well-*informed* opinion—that nineteenth-century liberal theorists had in mind.

In between, there is "opinion" in a third sense: opinion that is not wholly unformed but that is nevertheless clearly not based on any real depth of conviction. A person holding such an opinion may hold it over a considerable period of time; he may be able to give one or two reasons for holding it; he may even from time to time speak as though he feels strongly about it. But in fact, like the person answering the pollster's questions more or less randomly, the person holding such an opinion has probably not thought a great deal about the matter at hand and probably does not feel strongly about it. In all likelihood, it would not take a great deal to make him change his mind. A person in this position can reasonably be said to have an opinion; but his opinion is underdeveloped, ill formed. As a matter of fact, most people's opinions on most middle-range political issues most of the time probably approximate to this model.

What was the nature of the British public's opinions about the European Community? There certainly did seem to be a preponderance of opinion one way or the other on the issue during most of our period. The majorities in favor were very large in 1960 and again in 1965 and 1966; the majorities against were very large during much of 1970 and 1971. Only very seldom did opinion seem to be evenly divided. Moreover, despite the frequent changes of attitude on the part of the Labour party, most voters were capable of perceiving, at any given moment, which of the major parties was the more pro-European. For example, in mid-November 1966, National Opinion Polls (NOP) asked voters which of the two major parties they thought was keenest on joining the Common Market. Only a few days before, Harold Wilson, a Labour prime minister, had announced in the House of Commons that the government would shortly be initiating exploratory talks aimed at eventual British EEC membership. Yet 48 percent of NOP's respondents believed, correctly, that the Conservatives were in reality the keener of the two parties on the issue, and only 16 percent thought that Labour was keener; the remaining 36 percent thought there was no difference between the parties or were "don't knows."[5] Much later, in July 1971, NOP asked voters about the current stand of the Labour party. A good deal of confusion in voters' minds might have been expected, since Labour, having applied for EEC membership while in Government, was now, in opposition, both internally divided on the issue and increasingly disposed to condemn the entry terms negotiated by the Conservatives. Nevertheless, fully 63 percent of those interviewed in the NOP poll believed, rightly, that Labour was against the Common Market or that it was divided "half and half," and, despite Wilson's frequent protestations that Labour would favor entry if only the right terms could be negotiated, only 20 percent believed that Labour was currently in favor of entry. In answer to another question, a majority of these same respondents indicated that they were aware that Labour had changed its view on Europe during the previous two years.[6]

Voters thus appeared to have opinions about Europe; they were certainly aware of what the parties' opinions were. Indeed, if the data quoted thus far were all that were available, we might be inclined to infer that Europe was—or was capable of becoming—an issue of high salience in British electoral politics. But the data quoted so far are not the only ones available, and other data suggest a quite different picture. They suggest that, insofar as most voters held opinions about Europe at all, these opinions were very lightly held. They were not based on a solid body of information or on deep-seated conviction; they were subject to extreme short-run fluctuations.

Most voters were aware of the European issue, of course; after the five or ten years of incessant attention paid to it by politicians and the media, they could hardly fail to be. But that most voters were not interested enough in the European Community to have found out much about it is suggested by an NOP survey conducted in June 1971—ten years after Macmillan's initial Common Market application and in the midst of the renewed Brussels negotiations that were shortly to prove successful.[7] The proportion of respondents disapproving of the country's joining the Common Market was more than double the proportion in favor: 58 percent to 26 percent, with 16 percent "don't knows." But the members of the sample were then asked, "Do you happen to know which European nations are

---

[5] *NOP Political Bulletin*, November 1966, p. 9.

[6] Ibid., July 1971, pp. 18, 19.

[7] Ibid., June 1971, p. 15.

full members of the Common Market? If yes, which?" Of the 1,867 voters in the sample, only 13 percent named all six EEC member countries correctly and no other; nearly double that number, 24 percent, could not identify—or at least did not identify—a single member state. The proportions mentioning each of the six countries were: France, 69; Germany, 56; Belgium, 42; Holland, 36; Italy, 34; Luxembourg, 22; others, 15. In other words, only two of the six member countries were named by majorities of respondents, and scarcely one-third of those interviewed knew that Italy was a member of the Common Market even though the treaty to which Britain was seeking to become a signatory was known as the Treaty of Rome.

By themselves, of course, these figure prove little. It is well known that "quiz" questions of the type used in the NOP survey tend to underestimate respondents' knowledge, and in any case it is perfectly possible for people to hold strong views about subjects about which they know little or nothing.[8] But many other surveys conducted during the period point in the same direction.

For example, two academic researchers, David Butler and Donald Stokes, interviewed a sample of respondents in the summer of 1963 and again, some eighteen months later, in the autumn of 1964. The overall division of opinion on Europe was virtually unchanged between these two points in time. This seemingly stable overall division, however, concealed a pattern of individual change that was very fluid. Fully half of the Butler-Stokes sample conceded at either or both of the two interviews that they had no opinion about Europe; and, of those who did claim to have an opinion on both occasions, fewer than four-fifths on both occasions voiced the same opinion. In other words, fewer than two-fifths of the total sample in 1963–1964 had an opinion on Europe that was also stable. Butler and Stokes reject the hypothesis that the switches they observed represented large blocs of opinion moving in mutually cancelling directions. Rather, they conclude, "the most reasonable interpretation of the remarkable instability of responses is that Britain's policy towards the Common Market was in 1963–1964 a matter on which the mass public had formed attitudes to only a very limited degree."[9]

Butler and Stokes had the advantage of interviewing the same respondents on more than one occasion. There is no way of knowing

[8] The NOP question was open-ended. Jowell and Spence in 1974 asked a closed-ended question and found that a much larger proportion of respondents knew—or could guess—which were the EEC member states. See *The Grudging Europeans*, chapter 2, esp. p. 7.

[9] Butler and Stokes, *Political Change in Britain*, p. 279.

for certain whether the same pattern of response-uncertainty persisted into the late 1960s and early 1970s; but there is every reason to suspect that it did. For instance, the highest proportion ever recorded by the Gallup poll in favor of Europe was 71 percent; the lowest ever recorded was 35 percent. But these two figures were reported only eleven months apart, in July 1966 and June 1967.[10] It is a little hard to believe that, if most voters really had had well-formed opinions about Europe, so many of them would have changed their minds in so short a period. Four years later, in 1971, National Opinion Polls reported a fourteen percentage point decline in the number disapproving of EEC entry within the space of four weeks.[11] Again, the figures imply the existence of unformed attitudes rather than of meaningful attitude change.

Another indication that Europe was not a high-salience issue for most voters is provided by the answers to the question, frequently asked by National Opinion Polls, "What do you think is the single most important problem facing Great Britain today?" If many voters had felt strongly about it, the Common Market ought to have loomed large in the responses to this question, especially at times when Common Market negotiations were pending or in progress. But it did not. The issues mentioned most frequently over the years—often by as many as 50 or 60 percent—were the cost of living, unemployment, strikes, and the troubles in Northern Ireland. The proportion mentioning the Common Market usually ran at between 4 and 8 percent and never reached 15 percent. Indeed on only four occasions, all between the summer of 1970 and the spring of 1972, did the number mentioning Europe exceed 10 percent.[12] If the NOP question had been phrased in more personal, less abstract terms, the number mentioning Europe might well have been even smaller.

In sum, then, most British voters, if asked by the opinion polls between 1961 and 1973 whether or not they were in favor of Britain's joining the Common Market, were capable of giving a response. The proportion of "don't knows" was perhaps a little on the high side (see Table 2-1), but after 1966 it seldom exceeded 20 percent. But these figures were misleading. They implied a higher level of attitude formation, and stronger feelings about the issue, than actually existed. Most voters knew little about Europe and cared less. The cost of living, unemployment, and strikes were issues for "us"—concrete, personal, likely to have a direct bearing on the lives of individuals.

---

[10] *Gallup Political Index*, July 1966, June 1967.

[11] *NOP Political Bulletin*, June 1971, p. 14; July 1971, p. 3.

[12] *NOP Political Bulletin, passim.*

Table 2-2
RESPONSES TO QUESTION "DO YOU APPROVE OR DISAPPROVE OF BRITAIN JOINING THE COMMON MARKET?" BY CLASS, SEX, AND AGE
(in percentages)

| | Social Class [a] | | | | Sex | | Age | | | | | |
	AB	C1	C2	DE	Male	Female	18-24	25-34	35-44	45-54	55-64	65+
Approve	62	50	33	26	46	34	47	43	43	41	32	32
Disapprove	26	32	49	54	40	45	38	40	41	42	47	47
Don't Know	12	18	18	20	14	21	15	17	16	17	21	21

[a] This fourfold classification, used by National Opinion Polls and other British market research organizations, is based on occupation. The AB category comprises professional, managerial, and administrative workers, the C1 category routine nonmanual workers, the C2 category skilled manual workers, and the DE category semi-skilled and unskilled manual workers, pensioners, and the unemployed.
Source: *NOP Political Bulletin*, March 1972, p. 6.

Europe by contrast was an issue for "them"—a politicians' issue, abstract, remote, having little bearing on daily life. It is doubtful whether most politicians paid much attention to the opinion-poll findings on Europe or whether they analyzed them in these terms; but their own methods of tapping public opinion—ranging from formal meetings with constituents to casual conversations with taxi drivers—undoubtedly brought home the same message. Governments could go their own way on Europe; they need not concern themselves overmuch with the electorate.

The data we have cited so far are enough to explain what happened between 1961 and Britain's entry into Europe in January 1973. If, however, we wish to understand what was to happen later, we need to push our analysis further. In particular, we need to know who was in favor of, and opposed to, British membership in the Common Market and also, if voters did hold opinions on Europe, why they held them.

The opinion poll reported in Table 2-2 has been chosen more or less at random from the many available. It happens to have been conducted in March 1972, at a time when views on the Common Market were fairly evenly divided; but it could have been conducted at almost any time between 1961 and 1973. As the table shows, the differences of opinion among the various sections of the electorate were quite considerable. In particular, the middle classes (classes AB and C1) favored Europe more than the working classes (C2 and DE),

Table 2-3

VOTERS SUPPORTING BRITAIN'S ENTRY INTO THE COMMON MARKET, BY PARTY, 1966-1973

(in percentage points)

Date of Survey	Labour voters [a] (1)	Conservative voters [a] (2)	Difference [b] (3)
July 1966	39	53	14
January 1967	44	38	6
May 1967	16	−18	34
June 1967	4	−10	14
November 1967	12	−17	29
July 1969	5	−25	30
November 1969	−20	−43	23
March 1970	−29	−49	20
November 1970	−45	−28	17
June 1971	−47	−9	38
September 1971	−31	20	51
April 1972	−37	42	79
August 1972	−36	32	68
November 1972	−35	28	63
January 1973	−26	38	64
October 1973	−48	17	65

[a] Proportion of voters in favor minus proportion against.
[b] Column 1 minus column 2.
Source: *NOP Political Bulletin.*

and men favored it more than women. Although almost no one noticed it at the time, what this meant in practice was that those who disapproved of Britain's Common Market membership were disproportionately concentrated in those sections of the electorate that are usually the least interested in politics and the least well informed about political issues. It probably follows, though there is no direct evidence on the point, that those disapproving of British membership had even less well developed attitudes on the Common Market than those in favor and were likely to be even more prone to changing their minds. In other words, there was reason to suppose, even in 1972, that anti-European opinion might in the long run prove "softer" than pro-European opinion—that it might more easily be eroded by the pressure of events.

Another important element in explaining the British public's attitudes towards Europe emerges from Table 2-3, which indicates how the supporters of the two major parties felt about Europe between mid-1966, when the Wilson Government first began to manifest a serious interest in Europe, and late 1973, by which time Britain was a member of the Common Market on terms that had been negotiated by the Heath Conservative Government and were being fiercely attacked by the Labour party. The table provides further evidence for the extreme instability of the electorate's opinions; among Conservative voters, for example, the number approving of Britain's Common Market application exceeded the number disapproving by fifty-three percentage points in July 1966, while by November 1969 the number who disapproved exceeded the number in favor by fully forty-three percentage points—a turnover of nearly 50 percent in little more than three years. But the table also indicates the large role that party attachments seem to have played in determining voters' attitudes towards the Common Market.[13] To be sure, there was a time, between late 1969 and mid-1971, when the Common Market was unpopular with both parties (though in differing degrees); but from the spring of 1967 onwards the pattern is clearly one of supporters of the governing party rallying behind the Government of the day in its bid for Common Market membership, while supporters of the opposition party rejected both the Government and the market. No one could know for sure in, say, the winter of 1973–1974 whether, if a Labour Government were returned to power and decided to support continued EEC membership, this pattern would reassert itself; but there was reason to suppose that, whereas Labour voters might well swing in favor of the market as they had done before, Conservative voters would be less likely than Labour voters had been to turn against it. It was, after all, a Conservative Government that had negotiated entry; Britain was now a member of the EEC; and the Conservative leadership was now much more publicly committed to membership than it had been in the 1960s.[14]

[13] The Common Market could, of course, have determined voters' party attachments; but there is no evidence that the causal arrow was pointing in this direction, and a good deal that it was not. For example, in July 1971 voters who believed that their party was in favor of joining the Common Market were much more likely to be pro-European than voters who believed that their party was neutral or hostile; see *NOP Political Bulletin*, July 1971, p. 4. The fact that the parties—the Labour party in particular—changed their positions on Europe so often may well have made it especially difficult for voters to develop strong, lasting views on the matter.

[14] It should be noted that the Conservative and Labour supporters whose attitudes are reported in Table 2-3 were not, through time, the same people. Quite apart from deaths and comings of age, some of the Conservative voters of, say, 1967 were undoubtedly among the Labour supporters of, say, 1971. Given the transfer of support that took place from the Conservatives to Labour between 1967-1968, when the fortunes of the Labour party were at their nadir, and

Table 2-4

REASONS FOR APPROVING AND DISAPPROVING OF BRITAIN'S JOINING THE COMMON MARKET

Responses	Percentage
Reasons for Approving of Joining EEC	
Good thing for Britain/things would improve (unspecified)	32
Good for trade/exports with Europe, Common Market/ less import duties	30
Greater market for exports/for products/more competition/more employment	25
Closer alliance with Europe/more say in their internal politics	13
Not strong enough alone/must have stronger backing to survive	10
Reasons for Disapproving of Joining EEC	
Cost of living prices would rise/prices too high	63
Food prices would rise/will hit the housewife/clothing prices would rise	34
No benefit to us/unnecessary/no point/won't do any good (unspecified)	15

Note: The question was open-ended. All responses offered by more than 10 percent of respondents are listed above. Respondents could offer more than one reason for approving or disapproving.
Source: *NOP Political Bulletin*, March 1971, pp. 7-8.

If Conservative voters remained true to the cause and Labour voters followed the pro-Common Market lead given by a new Labour Government, there would occur, of course, a massive movement of opinion in the pro-European direction.

The question still remains: insofar as public opinion was on balance anti-European between 1967 and 1973, why was it so? What did the people of Britain have against the Common Market? In particular, why did they seem so opposed to the Common Market after 1967, having apparently been so strongly in favor of it before then?

The answer, disconcertingly simple, is contained in the bottom half of Table 2-4. When an issue is as remote as Europe was from the personal experience and understanding of the great majority of voters, not only are their opinions likely to be relatively unformed

1971-1973, when Labour's fortunes had improved somewhat, it may well be that some of the Conservative hostility to the Common Market reported in Table 2-3 is simply a byproduct of ex-Labour voters' having become temporary Conservative supporters in the late 1960s. In any case, it is worth noting that Conservative hostility to the Common Market was never as great, in terms of sheer numbers, as that on the Labour side.

and therefore highly volatile, but large numbers of voters are likely to seize upon, and to be much impressed by, any new information that enables them to make sense of the issue—to understand the unfamiliar in terms of the familiar, the unknown in terms of the known. The new information may be unimportant in itself; it may be misleading as regards the issue as a whole. Its importance lies not in itself but in how it is interpreted. Such new information was introduced into the Common Market debate early in 1967.

In the early months of 1967, politicians of all parties began to acknowledge that, if Britain were to join the Common Market, because of the workings of the Community's Common Agricultural Policy, the cost of living in Britain would rise sharply. Food prices would be especially affected. Until this point, if the benefits of joining the Common Market had seemed somewhat hazy to most people, so had the costs; but from early 1967 onwards, as Table 2-4 shows, whereas the benefits remained diffuse in most people's minds, even in the minds of those in favor of joining the EEC, the costs were seen as specific and immediate. "The country" might in some general way be better off if Britain joined the Common Market; but the individual citizens of the country would, in a very specific way, be worse off. The survey reported in the table was taken in March 1971; but every opinion poll reported similar findings during the whole 1967–1973 period. In an era of wage restraint and gradually accelerating inflation, the polls consistently found that more than 90 percent of respondents believed that food prices would go up if Britain went into Europe.[15] Clearly, if the European issue were ever put to the test, the pro-Europeans would have to find some way of countering, or at least neutralizing, the effects of this factor.

Most British voters, then, did not have strong views about the Common Market. They were disposed to take their cues on the Market from the political party they currently supported. The majority of them worried that Market membership would lead to higher prices. One thing is quite clear. The British people showed no enthusiasm whatever for the cause of building a united Europe.

---

[15] See for example NOP Political Bulletin, July 1971, pp. 14, 15. Asked whether they agreed or disagreed with a number of statements about British membership in the EEC, fully 94 percent of respondents agreed with the statement that food prices would rise. Asked in what ways they thought the Common Market would be bad for them personally, 68 percent of these same respondents, replying to an open-ended question, cited increases in the cost of living (see the same number of the Bulletin, p. 9). Asked what benefits the Market would bring, respondents usually gave very vague answers—"better standard of living," "better life for our children"—or no answer at all.

Table 2-5
RESPONSES TO QUESTIONS ABOUT EUROPEAN INTEGRATION ASKED IN SEVEN COUNTRIES, 1970
(in percentages)

Q: Assuming that Britain [joined the Common Market], would you be for or against the evolution of the Common Market towards the political formation of a United States of Europe?

	Holland	Luxem-bourg	West Germany	France	Belgium	Italy	EEC	Britain
For	64	75	69	67	60	60	65	30
Against	17	5	9	11	10	7	9	48
Don't know	19	20	22	22	30	33	26	22

Q: Would you be in favour of or against the election of a European parliament by direct universal suffrage; that is, a parliament elected by all the voters in the member countries?

	Holland	Luxem-bourg	West Germany	France	Belgium	Italy	EEC	Britain
In favor	59	71	66	59	56	55	59	25
Against	21	10	9	15	11	6	11	55
Don't know	20	19	25	26	33	39	30	20

Q: Would you be willing to accept, over and above your own government, a European government responsible for a common policy in foreign affairs, defense and the economy?

	Holland	Luxem-bourg	West Germany	France	Belgium	Italy	EEC	Britain
Willing	50	47	57	49	51	51	53	22
Not willing	32	35	19	28	19	10	20	60
Don't know	18	18	24	23	30	39	27	18

Source: Uwe Kitzinger, *Diplomacy and Persuasion* (London: Thames and Hudson, 1973), p. 33.

Table 2-5 speaks for itself. The British people did not want a United States of Europe, they did not want direct elections to a European parliament, they did not want a European government pursuing a European policy. In 1974 a study of British attitudes towards the Common Market was published under the title *The Grudging Europeans*. The title was well chosen.

3
THE LABOUR PARTY
AND EUROPE

The Labour party was deeply divided over Europe right from the beginning. Hugh Gaitskell's "thousand years of history" speech, setting out near-impossible conditions for British entry into Europe, was enthusiastically applauded at the party's annual conference in 1962; but already there existed in the party a band of strong pro-Europeans, and many of the subsequent speakers in the debate, including the party's then deputy leader, George Brown, vigorously dissented from Gaitskell's views. Five years later, the Wilson Government's motion approving Britain's new application for Common Market membership was passed by one of the largest majorities in parliamentary history, 488 to 62; yet 35 Labour M.P.s went into the lobbies against the Government and another 40 to 50 abstained. From June 1970 onwards, the gulf over Europe became so wide and deep that at times the entire party seemed in danger of being dragged down into it.

Opinion in the party was split roughly four ways. First, there were the staunch pro-Europeans, those for whom British entry into the Community was of paramount importance and who, whatever they said publicly, were prepared in practice to vote for entry almost no matter what the terms. These "Euro-fanatics," as their enemies called them, accounted for something like one-quarter of Labour M.P.s in the House of Commons. They had substantial, though minority, support in the trade unions. The third largest union in the country, for example, the National Union of General and Municipal Workers, with some 650,000 members, consistently supported the European cause.[1] In the early 1960s a few left-wing members of Parliament had favored British entry into Europe, but by the early 1970s all of them had changed their minds, ceased to be left wing, or retired from politics.[2] The pro-European M.P.s were thus, almost to a man, party moderates. Their leader was Roy Jenkins, who had risen rapidly during the time of the Labour Government, serving first as minister of aviation, then as home secretary, and finally as chancellor of the exchequer. A proud, aloof, somewhat shy man, Jenkins had a personality that was in itself to prove a factor in the internal party struggle.

The group furthest removed from the pro-Europeans—on almost all questions, not just on Europe—was the left wing of the party, organized in Parliament in the so-called Tribune Group.[3] The Tribune Group, like the pro-Europeans, numbered about one-quarter of the parliamentary Labour party. Its members were the lineal descendants of all of the various left-wing groupings and factions that had existed in the party since the late 1940s—Keep Left, the Bevanites, Victory for Socialism. Their philosophy was straightforwardly state-socialist and anticapitalist; on the Continent they probably would have been Communists or members of some left-wing splinter party. Their strength in the years immediately after 1970 lay largely in the trade unions, which were then going through a radical phase. The country's two largest unions, the Transport and General Workers' Union, with nearly 1,650,000 members, and the Amalgamated Union of Engineering Workers, with more than 850,000, consistently supported massive extensions of public ownership in industry and also consistently opposed British membership of the Common Market. The Tribune Group did not have a leader in quite the way that the pro-Europeans had; but their best-known spokesman was Michael Foot, a stalwart of the left for twenty-five years, a brilliantly effective parliamentarian,

---

[1] Very little research has been done into the politics of Britain's trade unions, and no one really knows why the various unions took the different lines on Europe that they did. Two books on the unions, which throw some light on their politics, are Innis Macbeath, *Cloth Cap and After* (London: George Allen & Unwin, 1973), and Stephen Milligan, *The New Barons: Union Power in the 1970s* (London: Temple Smith, 1976).

[2] For the names of some of them, see Stephen Haseler, *The Gaitskellites: Revisionism in the British Labour Party 1951-64* (London: Macmillan, 1969), p. 227, n. 1. The correlation between being left-wing and being anti-European gradually increased. By 1975 only one declared left-winger, Paul Rose, the M.P. for Manchester, Blackley, was still a member of the pro-European camp.

[3] The Tribune Group is named after the left-wing weekly paper *Tribune*. There exists no good study either of the Tribune Group or of the Labour party's left wing generally.

34

and a waspish, acid-tongued platform orator. Foot was one of the most popular M.P.s among Labour's activists in the constituencies.

If, however, all of Labour's left-wingers were anti-Europeans, by no means all of its anti-Europeans were left-wingers. On the contrary, a substantial minority of the party's moderates were passionately hostile to Europe. Their number is hard to estimate since, unlike the pro-Europeans and the Tribune Group, they did not form a cohesive group; but there must have been about twenty of them in the House of Commons at any given time. They worked together with the left on the European issue—some of them enthusiastically, some of them less so—and their presence made it possible for the left to claim, with justice, that the European debate was not just another manifestation of the age-old struggle between right and left for the party's soul. The leading figures among the anti-European moderates were Douglas Jay, an economist, a leading party intellectual and a former senior cabinet minister, whose presence in the anti-European ranks did much to lend respectability to the cause, and Peter Shore, a younger man, who had served, though not with any great distinction, in Harold Wilson's cabinet from 1967 onwards. Both men were almost fanatical in their opposition to Europe; they also knew a great deal about it and were much the best informed of those in the anti-Europe camp. In the case of Shore, who gradually emerged as the more prominent of the two, even his opponents agreed that he greatly increased his stature by the way he comported himself during the anti-EEC campaign.

These three groups—the pro-Europeans, and the left-wing and moderate anti-Europeans—accounted for rather more than half of Labour M.P.s and probably for rather more than half of the party in the country. But there was a fourth group, to which it is hard to attach a label. These were the M.P.s who may have been mildly in favor of Britain's going into Europe, or may have been mildly against, or may not have had any views one way or the other, but who did not believe that Europe was an issue of overriding importance and who were more concerned with the maintenance of party unity than with achieving any particular outcome on Europe. These were the M.P.s most prone to follow a pro-European lead if it were given by a Labour Government, most prone to be hostile if the Conservatives were in power. Such M.P.s were likely to be particularly sensitive to the views of the party conference and of their own constituency activists; they were also likely to be sensitive to the moods of public opinion. They were apt to claim that the precise terms of Britain's Common Market entry mattered to them—that they would be in favor of entry on the right terms, against it on the wrong ones. This group was crucial. It ultimately held the balance of power in the party. To it, as it happened, belonged the two leading figures in the party: Harold Wilson and James Callaghan. We shall return to their role shortly.

It is, however, one thing to identify the groups that existed in the party, quite another to explain why the members of the various groups held the views that they did. All of the parties to the debate advanced arguments, of course—about the balance of payments, about the balance of power in Europe, about the prospects for economic growth, about all sorts of things—and in some cases the arguments that an individual advanced may have constituted his real motives. Reg Prentice, for example, one of the party's most outspoken moderates, felt strongly about the need for Britain to increase the amount of its aid to underdeveloped countries. He was anti-European when the Community appeared inward-looking, a rich man's club; but he gradually became pro-European as it emerged that the Six were spending more on overseas aid than Britain, and as it became clear, too, that Britain's chronic economic weakness meant that the country could not spend a great deal more on aid even if it wanted to.[4]

But no one listening to the Labour party's Common Market debate in the sixties and early seventies can have escaped the feeling that, for most of the participants, the arguments that they advanced were only part of the story—and not always a very large part. What was said in the debate was often true and important, but often it amounted to no more than a thin surface covering a much deeper well of emotion. The debate, for one thing, was frequently far more passionate than its substance could possibly have warranted; the most obscure details of the Community's agricultural policy were disputed with a quasi-religious fervor. More significant still, over a period of fourteen years the world changed, and the nature of the arguments appropriate to the debate changed with it; but the great majority of the disputants on both sides clung tenaciously to their original positions. The pro-Europeans began by emphasizing the fillip that EEC membership would give to the British economy; when that argument, after the 1973 oil crisis, no longer seemed very plausible, they were forced back onto claiming that, if Britain were outside the EEC, it would suffer a real decline in living standards. The anti-Europeans began by emphasizing their devotion to the Common-

---

4 On Prentice, see Penniman, *Britain at the Polls*, pp. 31, 199.

wealth. As the Commonwealth declined in importance, however, the anti-Europeans did not become more pro-European. Rather, they largely dropped the Commonwealth argument and picked up others that seemed ready to hand—attacks on the "Brussels bureaucracy" for example. Many of the arguments used in the debate, in other words, were but weapons in a war; they were not really the cause of the war.

What was the cause? Among the anti-Europeans, two emotions predominated. The left-wing, Tribune Group anti-Europeans were moved more by one of them, the moderates more by the other. The left-wingers were seized of an idea that has already been referred to briefly in Chapter 1: the idea that the countries of the Six were somehow inherently "capitalist" and that, if Britain joined the EEC, it would be joining a capitalist power bloc from which it could never escape.[5] They were similarly convinced that Common Market membership was in the interests of the British capitalist class and therefore could not be in the interests of British workers. To read the debates on Europe at the Labour party's annual conferences over the years is to be half-submerged in the rhetoric of revolutionary socialism and the class war:

> There should be no doubt about the purposes of the Common Market. It is an attempt by European capitalist organisations to maintain the exploitation and to perpetuate the exploitation of capitalism on a European scale.

> I do not take on good faith the intentions of a capitalist system dominated mainly by right-wing Governments in Europe.

> I am sure the British working class do not wish to associate themselves with the group of Europeans which is dominated by capitalists.

> The Treaty of Rome is a betrayal of socialism.[6]

For the left-wing anti-Europeans, the Common Market meant the end of a dream—the dream of building a socialist Jerusalem in England's green and pleasant land.

---

[5] See above, p. 4.

[6] The party conference reports contain a wealth of such remarks. The ones quoted above were chosen more or less at random. The specific references are, in order: *Report of the Sixty-First Annual Conference of the Labour Party*, p. 167; *Report of the Sixty-Sixth Annual Conference of the Labour Party*, Scarborough, 1967 (London: Labour party, 1967), p. 271; *Report of the Seventieth Annual Conference of the Labour Party*, Brighton, 1971 (London: Labour party, 1971), pp. 118, 136.

Most of the anti-European moderates were probably not much swayed by this kind of rhetoric. "Capitalism" as a symbol did not mean much to them; they accepted the mixed economy. Their motives ran deeper still, and in some respects were more difficult to acknowledge publicly. The fact is that, like many Conservative opponents of the Common Market, they could not bear the idea of foreigners making decisons affecting the lives of ordinary British citizens; they could not bear the idea that Britain no longer had a large role to play in world affairs. Theirs, though they would have denied it, was the politics of imperial nostalgia, of xenophobia mixed occasionally with anti-Catholicism. "I did not come into Socialist politics in this country . . .," Peter Shore told the 1972 party conference, "to connive in the dismantling of the power of the British people as represented in their Parliament and in their Government."[7] The anti-European moderates often had close ties with the Commonwealth and also the United States; for many of them, psychologically, Mannheim and Milan were much further away than Delhi or even Des Moines. Few of the anti-Europeans spoke a foreign language; one of them, it was alleged, when he traveled abroad always carried his own food with him in little plastic bags.[8] If for the left-wingers the Common Market meant the end of their dream of socialism, for the anti-European moderates it meant admitting that Britain was just another country, one among many in the modern world—and not one of the richest or most powerful.

The anti-Europeans, in one way or another, resisted the modern world; the pro-Europeans, by contrast, accepted it. They accepted

---

[7] *Report of the Seventy-First Annual Conference of the Labour Party*, Blackpool, 1972 (London: Labour party, 1972), p. 205.

[8] Kitzinger, *Diplomacy and Persuasion*, p. 324. The reference was almost certainly to Douglas Jay. Kitzinger records on the same page the story of the Labour M.P. who, on the eve of his first visit to the Council of Europe, asked apprehensively, "And tell me—is there much vice in Strasbourg?" Hugh Dalton, the postwar chancellor of the exchequer and a moderate on issues other than Europe, was on Europe another passionate anti. George Brown in his memoirs quotes him as saying, "My boy, the right thing to do is to cut down the population of Britain to 26 millions by sending all the others away on assisted emigration, and then we could live happily and not have to get tangled up with a lot of bloody foreigners." *In My Way: The Political Memoirs of Lord George-Brown* (London: Victor Gollancz, 1971), p. 208. Lest, however, American readers assume that there is something peculiarly British about these attitudes they should remember the story of the two towns of Champagne and Urbana in Illinois. Champagne and Urbana are, topographically and economically, one town; they are divided only by a main street. In the early 1960s a referendum was held in each of the two towns to decide whether they should merge. In both towns the merger proposal was defeated. The citizens of each town are still foreigners in the other.

the mixed economy; they accepted, however reluctantly, the division of Europe; they accepted the fact of Britain's economic and political decline. They believed that, outside Europe, this decline would be accelerated; they believed that, inside it, it might be reversed. The pro-Europeans were especially conscious of the importance for the peace of Europe of the drawing together of France and Germany. It was largely for this reason that the pro-Europeans' ranks included a substantial number of older M.P.s, many of whom had had contacts with Continental socialists before the war or had served on the Council of Europe in its early days.[9] The pro-Europeans not only accepted the modern world: by and large, they liked it and wanted to embrace it. They did not mind Britain giving up some of its "sovereignty"; on the contrary, they were exhilarated by the idea of the leaders of different nations meeting together to try to solve their common problems. The pro-Europeans were internationalists in spirit. They were deeply worried about the effect on the British as a people if they were made to turn in upon themselves. As one prominent pro-European put it in the House of Commons:

> Like many others, I became a Socialist through an awareness of injustice and human suffering, but my own vision then, 30 years ago, was more than fine new flats and health centres and schools and jobs for all and fewer accidents in the Liverpool docks. Physical changes, satisfying material needs, a new environment—these were only steps towards a greater liberation.
>
> I do not say for a moment that these objectives are not shared by many of those who take a different view on this issue. My point is simply that if we stand back from Europe, saying that the risk is too great, the consequences for our national life will be much wider. When opportunities are refused and vision withers, bitterness and cynicism take their place. That is not my sort of Britain. I did not come into politics to help create it. And it is not what I want for my children.[10]

---

[9] Indeed Labour M.P.s aged sixty and over were more likely to be pro-European than younger M.P.s. See the analysis of the vote in the House of Commons on October 28, 1971, in Kitzinger, *Diplomacy and Persuasion*, Appendix 1, pp. 400-5. George Brown describes the early days of the Council of Europe and the effect that attending the Council had on him in *In My Way*, pp. 206-7.

[10] *Parliamentary Debates* (Hansard), House of Commons, vol. 823, October 21, 1971, col. 950. The speaker was William Rodgers who later, in the spring of 1976, was to help organize Roy Jenkins's unsuccessful bid for the party leadership.

The divisions in the party were thus not just divisions over a policy. They were divisions of ideology, of political outlook, even of personal temperament. It was not certain after 1970 that the party could survive them.

The formal position when Labour left office in June 1970 was reasonably clear. The outgoing Labour Government was committed to British EEC membership; indeed, as we saw in Chapter 1, a date had already been agreed for the opening of negotiations between Britain and the Six.[11] No one doubted that the negotiations would be conducted in good faith by both sides and that, given time, they would succeed. Had Labour won the June 1970 election, Harold Wilson, not Edward Heath, would today be known as the man who took Britain into Europe. The Labour party, as a party, was equally committed—or so it appeared. In the 1967 House of Commons vote approving the Government's pro-EEC policy, although 35 Labour members voted against the Government and 40 to 50 others abstained, the Government had the support of fully 260 M.P.s on the Labour side—three-quarters of the parliamentary party. Likewise in 1967, the party's annual conference accepted by a more than two-to-one majority a statement by the National Executive Committee (NEC) fully supporting the Labour Government's EEC application.[12]

But the appearances were misleading, and between June 1970 and the autumn of 1972 all of the Labour party's main institutions— the National Executive, the annual conference, and the party in Parliament—one by one came to occupy a position which, while it never rejected British membership of the Common Market outright, was so vehement in its oppositon to the terms of entry negotiated by the Conservatives, and laid down such rigorous conditions for any cooperation between a future Labour Government and the Common Market, as to amount to rejection of the whole idea of membership—if not in principle then certainly in practice.

The slide from the commitment to Europe began immediately after the general election and accelerated rapidly. At the October 1970 annual conference, at a time when the Conservative Government's negotiations with the Six in Luxembourg were only just beginning, the National Executive succeeded in carrying a motion reaffirming the party's European policy; but another motion calling for opposition to Common Market membership on any terms that

---

[11] See above, p. 22.

[12] The statement, "Labour and the Common Market," is printed as Appendix 3 to the *Report of the Sixty-Sixth Annual Conference of the Labour Party*, pp. 329-32.

the Conservatives might conceivably obtain was only narrowly defeated.[13] A few weeks later it was decided to hold a special party conference on the European issue in the following summer. By the time the special conference met, in London in July 1971, the entry terms negotiated by the Government were known. No vote was taken at the conference, but Harold Wilson, winding up the debate, made it clear that he personally rejected the Conservatives' terms; he denied heatedly that the terms negotiated by the Conservatives would have been acceptable to a Labour Government: "It is irresponsible for anyone who knows the facts to assert otherwise."[14] Eleven days later, the National Executive, which was by now swinging sharply to the left, announced its opposition to entry on the Tory terms and called on the parliamentary Labour party "to unite wholeheartedly in voting against the Government's policy." At the party's regular conference in October, the Executive's view was accepted by an overwhelming majority. Another resolution, calling for the withdrawal of Britain's EEC application, whatever the terms, was defeated; but already, in a little over a year, the party had shifted from a robust pro-Europeanism—at least in terms of its formal pronouncements—to something approaching à outrance opposition.[15]

The same process that was occurring outside Parliament was also occurring inside. In the early months of 1971, 132 Labour M.P.s —nearly half of the parliamentary party—signed a House of Commons motion stating that "entry into the EEC on the terms so far envisaged would be against the interests of this country."[16] When

---

[13] The vote was 3,049,000 to 2,954,000. See the Report of the Sixty-Ninth Annual Conference of the Labour Party, Blackpool, 1970 (London: Labour party, 1970), pp. 188, 200.

[14] Report of the Seventieth Annual Conference of the Labour Party, p. 355. Wilson felt constrained to make this denial because several of his foreign ministers—notably Roy Jenkins, Michael Stewart, the former foreign secretary, and George Thomson, who was in charge of negotiations with the EEC under Wilson—were saying precisely the opposite: that the terms negotiated by the Conservatives, although not ideal, would have been acceptable to a Labour cabinet. George Thomson, in his speech to the special conference (pp. 322-23), said that he would have advised a Labour cabinet to accept the terms negotiated by the Conservatives, and added: "Looking back over my experience of these negotiations as conscientiously as I can and objectively as I can, my personal judgment is that if we had won the Election and had still been facing the realities, the responsibilities and limitations of government, these terms would have gone through a Labour Cabinet." Michael Stewart's speech (p. 350) amounted to a personal attack on Wilson for having changed his position.

[15] For the terms of the National Executive's resolution, see Report of the Seventieth Annual Conference of the Labour Party, pp. 114-15.

[16] Kitzinger, Diplomacy and Persuasion, p. 297.

Parliament took its vote on the Government's terms on October 28 of the same year, the bulk of the parliamentary party, 198 members, voted with Wilson to reject the Tories' terms. But no fewer than 69 Labour members, led by Roy Jenkins, Brown's successor as the party's deputy leader, defied both the party conference and a three-line whip to go into the division lobbies with the Conservative Government; another twenty pro-European M.P.s abstained.[17] The rebellion was of a type, and on a scale, unprecedented in the party's history. Not only did the deputy leader defect; he took with him into the lobbies three other members of the shadow cabinet, Harold Lever, George Thomson, and Shirley Williams, and the chairman of the parliamentary Labour party, Douglas Houghton. A fourth member of the shadow cabinet, Anthony Crosland, abstained. Of the seventeen members of Wilson's 1970 cabinet who were still in the House of Commons, only nine now voted with him. The rebels included some of the longest-serving Labour M.P.s (one of them had first been elected in 1929); they also included a large proportion of the party's most talented younger members—men and women who would almost certainly have to be included in any future Labour Government. "Rebellion" is too weak a word for what happened on October 28. This was civil war.[18]

---

[17] The terms "three-line whip" and "division lobbies" perhaps need explaining for American readers. Each week every M.P. representing one of the major parties receives through the post a document informing him of the parliamentary business for the following week, and also informing him of the degree of importance attached to each item of business by the leadership of his party. This document is known as "the whip." Items of business not considered at all important by the party leaders are underlined only once. Items of business considered more important are underlined twice. Items of business considered very important are underlined three times. Hence "three-line whip." The force of a three-line whip is to require the M.P. to be present and also to vote in the way determined by his party. In other words, the October 28 rebels were defying the most forceful instruction that their party could give them. The "division lobbies" in the British House of Commons are simply the two lobbies or antechambers—one for the "ayes" and one for the "noes"—through which members file to record their votes. There are voice votes in the British House of Commons, but there are no roll-call votes, nor are there voting machines.

[18] The war was fought, however, at least within the parliamentary party, without any ultimate weapons being used. It was significant for what was to happen later that Wilson made it clear that, although he deplored the action of the rebels, especially the rebels from within the shadow cabinet, no further action was to be taken against them. See below, pp. 64-67. The shadow cabinet's tacit agreement to differ in 1971 made it easier for the actual cabinet to agree to differ in 1975. Again, see below, pp. 104-5. After the changes of September 1976, James Callaghan's Labour cabinet contained twenty-two members sitting in the House of Commons. Of these twenty-two, six had voted with the Conservatives and against their own party on October 28, 1971, and another two had abstained.

The war was, however, being won, at least in the short term, by the anti-Europeans. In defying a three-line whip to the extent not merely of abstaining but of voting with the Conservative Government, many of the pro-European rebels had put at risk their political careers.[19] They could rebel once; they could not safely go on rebelling. Thus, during the passage through the House of Commons of the European Communities Bill during the following year, the great majority of the pro-European M.P.s joined, very reluctantly, with their anti-Market colleagues in trying night after night to vote down the bill's detailed provisions. A leading pro-European had predicted: "1971 was a difficult year; 1972 will be a distasteful one."[20] Most pro-European M.P.s indeed found 1972 very distasteful. But, fortunately for them, a few of their number, including several members who planned to retire at the next election, were prepared if need be to abstain in any divisions on the bill that seemed likely to be close, in order to maintain the Government's majority. In the end, one member of this "kamikaze squad," as it came to be called, abstained 102 times, another 98, another 88. The bill as a result was never really in danger.[21]

It was not enough, however, for the majority in the party simply to oppose the Conservatives' terms and to seek to defeat the Government's bill. It seemed highly probable that the bill would become law and that, by the time a Labour Government were returned to office, Britain would be a member of the EEC—and might possibly have been a member for quite some time. What was a Labour Government to do under these circumstances? The answer was first suggested as early as September 1971 by James Callaghan, then the party's spokesman on employment matters. It was a simple answer and managed to make some sense of Labour's strange stance of approving entry into Europe in principle but objecting in practice to the Conservatives' terms—and indeed to any terms that were

[19] The risk was a real one. At least one M.P., Dick Taverne, the member for Lincoln, was ousted by his constituency Labour party as a direct consequence of his rebellion on Europe, and another, Dick Leonard, the member for Romford, found it impossible to find another constituency after Romford, as the result of a redistribution, had been turned from a safe Labour seat into a safe Conservative one. On the Taverne affair, see Dick Taverne, The Future of the Left: Lincoln and After (London: Jonathan Cape, 1974), and Austin Ranney, "Selecting the Candidates," in Penniman, ed., Britain at the Polls, pp. 56-58.

[20] Quoted in Kitzinger, Diplomacy and Persuasion, p. 390. See the whole of chapter 13 for a detailed account of the passage of the European Communities Bill through Parliament.

[21] For details, see Kitzinger, Diplomacy and Persuasion, pp. 388-90. Chapter 6 in the same book describes the divisions within the Conservative party.

likely to be obtained by any Government. In a speech at Bradford, Callaghan warned Heath that he should be under no illusion that the issue would be closed forever by the result of the House of Commons vote in October:

> Both he and the Community should be aware that the issue will remain an open one until a general election has decided it. Even if Mr. Heath has his way about taking us in— nevertheless, when a Labour Government wins the confidence of the people, then it should be its intention to renegotiate, on a government-to-government basis, those terms which at the time will have been found objectionable and harmful to the interests of the British people.[22]

The key word was "renegotiate." And the idea that renegotiation was the best way forward was quickly taken up within the party. Wilson referred to it in his speech during the parliamentary debate in October 1971, and at Labour's annual conference the following year it became official party policy. A statement by the National Executive Committee, approved by the party conference, declared Labour's willingness to renegotiate; but it added, ominously: "If [the] renegotiations do not succeed, we shall not regard the Treaty obligations as binding upon us."[23] It was a measure of how far the party had come since the election that the same annual conference, in October 1972, passed, by 3,335,000 votes to 2,867,000,[24] an additional motion calling on any future Labour Government to withdraw

---

[22] Quoted in David Butler and Uwe Kitzinger, *The 1975 Referendum* (London: Macmillan, 1976), p. 16.

[23] *Report of the Seventy-First Annual Conference of the Labour Party*, p. 383. Wilson's speech in the House of Commons is quoted by Kitzinger, *Diplomacy and Persuasion*, p. 372.

[24] The large numbers of votes cast for and against this motion (and for and against other motions at Labour party conferences) are accounted for by the fact that the conference delegation of each organization affiliated to the party— mainly trade unions and constituency parties—casts as many votes as the organization has affiliated members. For example, a trade union with, say, 500,000 members might decide to affiliate 400,000 of them to the Labour party. The union's conference delegation would then cast 400,000 votes. Trade unions could, if they wanted to, divide their votes, casting, say, 300,000 votes one way and 100,000 the other; but in practice all of the unions affiliated to the Labour party cast "block votes," all of their votes being cast one way or the other. For each member that a union affiliates to the party, it has to pay to the party a small affiliation fee. For many years, the Transport and General Workers' Union has been not only the largest trade union in the country but also the union with the largest membership affiliated to the Labour party.

from the EEC unless the EEC abandoned, in effect, every one of its major economic policies.[25]

The slide from Europe considerably embarrassed the Labour party, which was pilloried in the press as irresponsible, inconsistent, and opportunistic. It evidently embarrassed Harold Wilson, who was repeatedly at pains to claim that, despite everything, he had not really shifted his position.[26] And it deeply divided Labour's leadership. Why, then, did it occur?

In the first place, the slide was perhaps not quite so precipitous as it seemed. There had always been a great deal of opposition to Europe in the party, and the two votes in 1967, in Parliament and at the party's annual conference, undoubtedly concealed the full extent of it. It was more than a straw in the wind that the 1967 conference, while endorsing the Labour Government's European initiative, at the same time cast more than 2,500,000 votes for an alternative resolution that, had it passed, would have sought to impose on the Government quite intolerable conditions. For example, it would have urged the Government "to give full and urgent consideration to alternative policies in close consultation with our Commonwealth and other trading associates throughout the world."[27] Wilson's success in carrying his party for Europe in 1967 in fact owed much to the simple fact that Labour was in power. It also owed much to the fact that the issue, as it was presented to the party in 1967, was still somewhat hypothetical. De Gaulle was still in

---

[25] *Report of the Seventy-First Annual Conference of the Labour Party*, pp. 197, 217. The resolution, moved by the Amalgamated Society of Boilermakers, Shipwrights, Blacksmiths and Structural Workers, is worth quoting in full: "This Conference declares its opposition to entry to the Common Market on the terms negotiated by the Tories and calls on a future Labour Government to reverse any decision for Britain to join unless new terms have been negotiated including the abandonment of the Common Agricultural Policy and the Value Added Tax, no limitations on the freedom of a Labour Government to carry out economic plans, regional development, extension of the Public Sector, Control of Capital Movement, and the preservation of the power of the British Parliament over its legislation and taxation, and, meanwhile, to halt immediately the entry arrangements including all payments to the European Communities, and participation in their Institutions in particular the European Parliament, until such terms have been negotiated, and the assent of the British electorate has been given." In other words, Labour was prepared to enter the church provided the church abandoned all of the holy sacraments and its belief in the divinity of Jesus Christ.

[26] For example, he devoted some five minutes of his speech to the 1971 special conference to refuting the charge that the party, and he personally, had been inconsistent on Europe. See *Report of the Seventieth Annual Conference of the Labour Party*, pp. 354-55.

[27] *Report of the Sixty-Sixth Annual Conference of the Labour Party*, p. 269. The vote, recorded on p. 286 of the conference report, was 3,536,000 to 2,539,000.

power, and serious negotiations with the EEC had not even begun. In 1967 a Labour M.P. could quite consistently cast his vote in favor of the British Government's making an application for EEC membership, while at the same time reserving his position with regard to the final outcome. Indeed such an M.P. was almost encouraged to do so by his own Government's insistence that, of course, it would sign the Treaty of Rome only if the terms were right. The Government's tough bargaining stance made it easy for even doubtful M.P.s to go along with it. By late 1971, however, all that had changed: Labour was no longer in power, the terms were known, the Treaty was about to be signed.

Not only was Labour no longer in power: the Conservative Government of Edward Heath was more deeply unpopular with Labour M.P.s, the trade unions, and the Labour rank and file generally than any Conservative Government had been since the 1930s. The Heath Government, in a particularly minatory style, was bringing in measure after measure that offended the sensibilities of Labour supporters and in some cases appeared to threaten their interests: the ending of free school milk in primary schools, an Industrial Relations Bill that alienated the unions, a Housing Finance Bill that alienated Labour local authorities and thousands of tenants in local council accommodation. The history of the Heath Government has been described in *Britain at the Polls*.[28] The point here is that it was extremely difficult for the trade unions and Labour M.P.s—opposed to the Government on everything else—to support it on Europe. Those who had no strong views on the matter—the fourth group described above—had no incentive to do so anyway; but even the pro-Europeans were placed in a peculiarly difficult position, since, if they did support the Government, they could be, and were, branded as traitors. Their position was not made any easier by the fact that the Government's overall majority in the House of Commons was quite small, under 30 in a House of 630 members. Since a minority of Conservative M.P.s were also opposed to Europe, there was always the possibility, however remote, that the Government could be brought down—but only if Labour was united in opposing it. So strong was the feeling that, when on February 17, 1972, the second

---

[28] See esp. Chapter 1. The "local authorities" referred to in the text are the British equivalent of American local governments (cities, and so on). "Local council accommodation" is what would be known in the United States as "public housing," except that far more Englishmen and Scotsmen than Americans live in such housing, with the result that the phrase "council housing" in Britain does not have quite the same connotations as "public housing" in the United States.

reading of the Government's European Communities Bill was carried only on the strength of Liberal votes, the Liberal leader, Jeremy Thorpe, was jostled in the Chamber by angry Labour members. The Labour chief whip—who was himself, rather surprisingly, a pro-European—went on record in the same month as saying, "I would do anything short of anarchy to bring this Government down."[29] Small wonder that pro-European sentiment lost ground in the party. It is perhaps surprising that so much of it remained.

And there was another factor, at least as important as either of the others. The twenty-eight months between the general election of June 1970 and the annual conference of October 1972 witnessed the most decisive shift to the left in the Labour party's history. The party's new statement of policy asserted that Labour's goal was to bring about a "fundamental and irreversible shift in the balance of power and wealth in favour of working people and their families." Its specific proposals included a wealth tax, the nationalization of building land, the municipalization of privately rented housing, the nationalization of the docks and the aircraft and shipbuilding industries, and the creation of a National Enterprise Board which would intervene massively in the workings of the private sector of industry.[30] This shift to the left was brought about by an increase in the number of left-wing Labour M.P.s and, more particularly, by a shift in the balance of power from right to left inside the trade unions. As the unions moved to the left, so too did the annual conference and the National Executive, both of which the unions, directly or indirectly, controlled.[31] The shift was caused in large part by the apparent failure of the moderate policies pursued by the 1964–1970 Wilson Government. The militants lost faith in the moderates; the moderates, to a considerable degree, lost faith in themselves. And many middle-of-the-road Labour M.P.s, sensing the way the wind was blowing, leaned with it rather than into it. The upshot was that the years 1970–1972 were particularly hard years for the moderates in the party and for the causes with which they were associated, including Europe. Labour's slide from Europe was thus part of a

[29] Kitzinger, Diplomacy and Persuasion, p. 386. The jostling incident is described on p. 388.

[30] Labour's Programme for Britain (London: Labour party, 1973). See also Penniman, ed., Britain at the Polls, pp. 17-18.

[31] A good indicator is provided by the composition of the women's section of the National Executive, which is elected by the whole of the annual conference—that is, in effect, by the trade unions. There are five members of this section. In the 1960s four of the five members were normally moderates; by 1972 only one of the five was a moderate.

general slide towards policies more extreme than any the party had known in the past.

All of the tensions in the Labour party during these years were inevitably channeled through the person of its leader for nearly ten years now, Harold Wilson. As the events just described unfolded, Wilson found himself partly a participant in them, but also partly a spectator. The leader of the Labour party, especially when the party is in opposition, has relatively few powers. He presides over the shadow cabinet; he makes appointments to the front bench; he can attend meetings of the National Executive, of which he is an *ex officio* member; he can speak from the platform at the annual conference; he can appear more or less as often as he wants on television. But, beyond that, he has few power resources. He can only, in the manner of an American president, try to persuade others that what he wants them to do on his responsibility is what they ought to want to do on their own.[32] The party leader can threaten, wheedle, cajole, maneuver; but he cannot control either the composition or the policies of any of the party's major organs. Moreover, Labour does not assign to its leader much in the way of pure "authority." It is not a custom in the Labour party that anyone should do anything simply because the leader wants him to. There is, if anything, an endemic suspicion of the party's leadership cadre. Wilson was, formally, the party's "leader," but his capacity to lead was in fact very limited.

Wilson felt the tensions in the party personally; he was also acutely conscious of them as political facts with which he would have to deal. It has sometimes been argued that he could have stopped the slide from Europe if he had really wanted to and if he had been prepared to take some personal risks to do so. It is just possible that he could. He might have provided a rallying point for the pro-European forces. He might have indicated that his personal commitment to Europe was so great that he would have to resign as leader if the party's decision went against him. But it is doubtful whether any actions of Wilson's could have prevented the party from adopting an increasingly anti-European line, and in any case it was not in his character to try to prevent it from doing so—or in his analysis of political realities. Instead he decided to play a subtler game, a waiting game. In time it was to prove brilliantly successful.

---

[32] For the presidential analogy, see Richard E. Neustadt, *Presidential Power: The Politics of Leadership* (New York: John Wiley, 1960), esp. chapter 3. It is also the case that a Labour party leader, like a Conservative party leader, is quite tightly constrained in the appointments that he makes, even when the appointments are formally in his gift. The appointments must be balanced in party terms; there are always some people who cannot be left out.

Wilson was not a pro-European by instinct. A provincial English-man by both background and temperament, he knew no foreign language and felt much more at home in Washington than in Paris or Bonn. He was, moreover, a patriot, who deeply regretted Britain's decline as a world power and could hardly reconcile himself to the idea that to be British prime minister was no longer to be one of the world's, or even Europe's, great movers and shakers. He was not at all happy to have climbed to the top of the greasy pole only to discover that it no longer afforded as good a view as it once had done. Wilson's was a world of fish and chips and HP sauce—a world that still regarded everything beyond the English Channel as foreign and "other." It was also the case that in 1971 and 1972 Wilson was a tired man. He was mentally and physically exhausted after leading the Labour party for the better part of ten years, and the general election defeat in 1970 had hurt him more than he cared to admit. He knew that Britain's future lay in Europe; he must have feared the consequences if a future Labour Government were to come to power irrevocably committed to taking Britain out of Europe. But he was not about to fight passionately in the cause of Europe—a cause that he believed in with his head, but not really with his heart. Anyway, he was confident that, somehow, everything would come right in the end.[33]

The political situation that confronted Wilson in his own party is not hard to analyze. In the first place, his own leadership was not entirely secure. The 1964–1970 Government had not been a great success, and he was widely blamed for its failures. He was blamed for the strained relations between the Labour party and the trade unions that resulted from the Labour Government's abortive effort to reform the unions in 1969.[34] He was also blamed by many for the loss of the 1970 election. He had once been thought to be the Labour party's greatest electoral asset. Not any longer. Moreover, there were at least two potential rivals waiting in the wings. Roy Jenkins, Wilson must have known, was constantly being urged to stand against him. And James Callaghan made no secret of the fact that, if the party wanted a new leader, he was available. Callaghan all but threw his hat into the ring in a well-publicized speech in Southampton in the early summer of 1971. He is said to have told a

---

[33] For further reflections on Wilson's leadership style, see Anthony King, "The Election that Someone Won—More or Less" in Penniman, ed., *Britain at the Polls*, pp. 178-79.
[34] See Peter Jenkins, *The Battle of Downing Street* (London: Charles Knight, 1970).

journalist who claimed that he, the journalist, could not leave London that night: "Well, if you want to hear the next leader of the Labour party, you'd better arrange to be there."[35]

It followed, since the anti-Europeans were a majority in the party, that Wilson could not take too many risks in offending them. One of his potential rivals, Callaghan, made it clear that he, at least, put the maintenance of party unity ahead of the Common Market. Indeed, under different circumstances, or had he been a different man, Wilson might have been tempted to throw in his lot with the anti-Europeans. But that option was not really open to him. For one thing, if he had done so, the charge that he had been inconsistent over Europe would have stuck; he would have been seen to have changed his view on one of the most important political questions of the day for no other purpose than to save his leadership. His political credit would have been destroyed—not least among the leaders of the other members of the Community, with whom he would have to work closely if he ever became prime minister again. Moreover, he did recognize, however reluctantly, that Britain's future lay within the Community.

Even in terms of the domestic political battle, it was not really in Wilson's interests to identify himself too closely with the anti-Marketeers. The pro-Europeans, as the 1971 vote in Parliament made clear, included several of the party's ablest and most widely respected leaders: Jenkins himself, George Thomson, Harold Lever, Shirley Williams. If they were driven out of the party, Labour's standing in the country would probably decline precipitously; it might even be hard for Wilson to form an effective future Labour cabinet. Moreover, Wilson's technique of leadership had always been a balancing technique. He knew that, if the moderates in the party became too powerful, as they had in the time of Gaitskell, there would be endless rows in the party; its unity would be jeopardized. But he also knew that, if the left became too powerful, Labour would stand little chance of winning the support of Britain's voters. His balancing technique contained, in addition, a personal element. Wilson was not wholly trusted by either wing of the party. He was well aware that, if he inclined too far in the direction of either, it would be in the interests of the other to try to displace him. To become the captive of one wing was to run the risk of becoming the victim of the other. In the early 1970s, Wilson was not about to run that risk.

He had therefore to devise a strategy that would preserve his

---

[35] Quoted in Kitzinger, *Diplomacy and Persuasion*, p. 300.

own personal position and at the same time retain a modicum of credibility for the party in the country. The strategy he chose was enormously complicated to execute, and inevitably entailed risks; but it was simple in essence. It contained three elements.

The first was that he must not allow any of his rivals to usurp his mantle as the preserver of the party's unity. He must at all times present himself as the greater uniter, the great mediator—above all of the factions because a member of none. Not only would such a posture help him to preserve his own position; it might enable him, with luck, to appeal successfully to the various warring factions to exercise a degree of restraint, not to smite the other side too hard in the heat of the battle. This first element in his strategy emerged clearly from a passage in his speech to the party's special conference in July 1971:

> At Newtown [a reference to an earlier speech] I referred to pressure. I made clear that all the pressures—or abuse—would not deflect me from my duty as Leader of this Party to recommend the course I believe right in the interests of Britain and our people. Nor from my duty— and I have always regarded this as the duty of the Leader— to do all in my power to maintain the unity of this Party. (*Applause.*) . . .
>
> I charge this Movement, as I have the right and duty to do, so to conduct this debate as to respect and honour the views of all members of the Party, and indeed of others, regardless of what those views may be. We must recognise that what divides us is an important policy issue, not an article of faith.[36]

What worried Wilson, of course, was that for many in the party Europe had in fact become precisely that—an article of faith.

The second element in Wilson's strategy was related to the first. Since he did not wish to see the pro-Europeans driven out of the party, and since he himself believed that Britain's destiny lay in Europe, he had in the end, whether he liked it or not, to defend the pro-Europeans' position, or at least to ensure that it was not rendered intolerable. Thus, his appeals for party unity were not— and were not meant to be—neutral as between the contending factions. They were meant to give aid and comfort to the pro-European side. After all, it was the pro-Europeans, who were in a minority in the party, and not the anti-Europeans, who needed the protection

---

[36] *Report of the Seventieth Annual Conference of the Labour Party*, pp. 359-60.

that these appeals provided. More than that, Wilson was determined that the party must on no account be allowed to reverse itself completely—to come out, in principle as well as in practice, against Common Market membership. If the party got itself into that position, then the position of the pro-Europeans would be completely undermined—and so would his own. He therefore made it his business to include in all of his numerous speeches—however anti-European they might be in tone—a restatement of his own, and the party's, ultimate European commitment. There can be little doubt that, in private, he warned the anti-Europeans of what the consequences would be if, in their enthusiasm, they tried to force the party as a whole to cross the thin line that divided opposition to Europe on the terms negotiated by the Tories—or likely to be negotiated by any other Government—from opposition to the concept itself.[37] Any number of caveats and conditions could probably be accommodated; an outright declaration of principle, Wilson knew, could not. He was thus in the positon of saying to the anti-Europeans, though never in so many words, "Thus far and no farther."

The third element in Wilson's strategy reinforced the second and was entirely in keeping with his character. It was to play for time. If matters were forced to an issue, the anti-European forces would win; the party would split. Therefore, matters must not be forced to an issue; the discussion must remain hypothetical; no one must be pinned down. Wilson's politics were the politics of movement. He always remembered what others in the party often seemed to forget: that the party was not in power; it was in opposition. The stakes in the party's internal battle were therefore not governmental decisions but forms of words—conference resolutions and NEC statements. And Wilson was not one to take mere words overseriously. After all, it might be years before the party returned to power, by which time Britain's EEC membership would be irreversible. Why tear the party apart now over something the party certainly could not control now, and might not even be able to control in the future? If the party were to return to power within a year or two, then it was even more important that the incoming Government's hands should not be tied. About the Common Market, as about so

---

[37] At the 1971 annual conference, for example, a resolution calling for the complete withdrawal of Britain's application to join the EEC failed to pass only because the Transport and General Workers' Union refused to vote for it—even though the union was anti-EEC. It is probable that Wilson was responsible for the union's exercising this degree of restraint. See Butler and Kitzinger, *The 1975 Referendum*, pp. 12-13.

many other things in life, time alone would tell. Harold Wilson was a great believer in time.

Rather surprisingly, Wilson seems at first to have overlooked another possible element in his strategy—the idea that the final decision on Europe might be shifted out of the party completely and placed in the hands of the electorate. How the Labour party—and, through it, the country—came to adopt the principle of holding a national referendum on the EEC we shall see in the next chapter.

4
THE DECISION TO HOLD
A REFERENDUM

Readers of this book must be beginning to wonder whether it is a book about the Common Market referendum or about the internal politics of the Labour party. The answer is that it has to be both. From the spring of 1972 onwards, the question of the referendum and the question of Labour's policy towards Europe were intertwined like the two strands of a double helix. Neither can be understood except in terms of the other. The decision to hold a referendum was a direct outcome of Labour's internal struggle over Europe. The Conservatives played almost no part in the decision. If the Conservatives had won the February 1974 general election, no referendum would have been held.

It is important to note that of course the question of whether a referendum should be held on a matter of major constitutional importance and the question of whether Britain should remain a member of the EEC are, logically, quite separate questions, raising quite different issues. The referendum question raises general issues in the field of democratic theory, concerning the proper relationship between governors and governed; the EEC question raises specific issues in the fields of foreign and economic policy, concerning the future of one country at one moment in time. So separate are the two questions that one should not, in logic, be able to infer an individual's views on either from his views on the other. The two questions should inhabit different worlds of discourse.

But they did nothing of the sort in the Britain of the early 1970s. On the contrary, once the question of holding a referendum on Europe began to be discussed as a serious possibility, to know that someone was anti-European was to know that he was in favor of holding a referendum; to know that someone was pro-European was to know that he was against holding one. The correlation between attitudes towards the referendum and attitudes towards Europe, which ought in logic to have approached zero, was in fact nearly perfect.

The reason was simple. As we saw in Chapter 2, the opinion polls after 1970 suggested that the majority of the electorate were opposed to British membership in the Common Market.[1] It seemed to follow that, if there were a popular vote on the issue, it would go against the Market. The anti-Europeans therefore wanted such a vote; the pro-Europeans did not want one. The referendum debate was simply an epiphenomenon of the Common Market debate. The two sides in the debate advanced all sorts of high constitutional arguments; but everyone knew that the M.P. or trade union leader who was arguing vehemently on one side of the debate would have been arguing just as vehemently on the opposite side if the opinion polls had been showing something different. It was just the sort of episode that gives the British on the Continent a reputation for perfidy, for being able to find highly moral justifications for performing wholly nonmoral acts.

There were individual exceptions, of course. One was the former Liberal leader, Jo Grimond, who believed in Europe but who also believed in direct democracy. Grimond supported the holding of a referendum even though he knew that it might mean Britain's withdrawing from Europe.[2] A more doubtful case was that of Tony Benn—who, more than any other individual, was responsible for Labour's taking up the referendum.[3] Benn was a popular figure in the Labour party and a leading member of its National Executive. He had served in the 1964–1970 Labour Government first as postmaster-general, then as minister of technology. He was undoubtedly a believer in direct democracy, in popular participation. As early as the spring of 1968, he could be heard advocating the widespread use of referenda in Britain, not necessarily in connection with the Common Market:

---

[1] See above, pp. 24-25.

[2] In 1969 Grimond voted in favor of a pro-referendum motion introduced by a Conservative M.P. named Bruce Campbell. See Philip Goodhart, *Referendum* (London: Tom Stacey, 1971), pp. 57-59, and Jo Grimond and Brian Neve, *The Referendum* (London: Rex Collings, 1975), esp. pp. 42-52, 106-25.

[3] Tony Benn began his political career as Anthony Wedgwood Benn but, presumably because such a double-barreled name sounded too aristocratic, given the political company that he was increasingly moving in, he began after 1970 to insist on being called simply Tony Benn. Students of political image-making are invited to consult Benn's entries over the years in the British *Who's Who*.

The five-yearly cross on the ballot paper is just not going to be enough. Inevitably we shall have to look again at the objections to the holding of referenda and see if they are still valid. . . .

If some real issues—perhaps for a start of the kind that are now decided by private Members' Bills—were actually put out for a decision in principle by a referendum, the situation would be transformed. . . . We might not like the result. But at any rate by sharing responsibility an interest in public policy would be stirred in every household.[4]

While still in government, Benn had been a consistent, if not notably enthusiastic, supporter of Britain's joining Europe, and he went on maintaining that he was, in principle, a pro-Marketeer for some time after the 1970 election. But Benn was also a very ambitious man, not given to flying in the face of majority opinion in his party. As the party's view hardened against accepting membership on the Tories' terms, so too did Benn's. It is hard to escape the suspicion that, even when he first proposed the holding of a referendum on Europe, he was already beginning to move in an anti-Market direction. Be that as it may, by the time the Common Market referendum actually took place, he was one of the most clamorous of the anti-Marketeers.

The first prominent Labour figure to put forward the possibility of a referendum specifically on Europe was not, as it happened, Tony Benn but someone who was already publicly committed as an anti-Marketeer—Douglas Jay. In an article in *The Times*, published only six weeks after the 1970 election, Jay argued that a decision to join the Common Market and sign the Treaty of Rome "would be a more drastic change in our constitution and the basic rights of the British people than any since power was given to the modern electorate in 1832." Parliament would be giving up a substantial part of its power to an outside body over which it could have little control. And the decision would be irreversible; Parliament could not bind its successors in theory, but in practice it was clear that, once such substantial powers had been given up, they could never be recovered. Under the circumstances, it would be a constitutional outrage if Parliament, in effect, abrogated both Britain's sovereignty and its independence without consulting the people directly.[5]

Jay's article attracted little attention. Labour was still committed

---

[4] Goodhart, *Referendum*, pp. 64-65.
[5] Douglas Jay, "Joining the Six—the case for a referendum," *The Times*, August 1, 1970.

to the Common Market and was still reeling from the blow of its election defeat. Nor did Benn attract a great deal more attention when he first advanced the same proposal—in an open letter to the voters of his constituency in November of the same year. He maintained that he personally was in favor of Britain's being a member of the Common Market, but then went on:

> If people are not to participate in this decision, no one will ever take participation seriously again. . . . It would be a very curious thing to try to take Britain into a new political unity with a huge potential for the future by a process that implied that the British public were unfit to see its historic importance for themselves.[6]

A motion in favor of a referendum was put by the Transport and General Workers' Union to Labour's National Executive in December 1970, but it was turned down almost without discussion. Similarly, at the October 1971 party conference, a union-sponsored amendment calling for a referendum was hardly mentioned in the general debate on the Common Market and was defeated by more than 2 million votes.[7]

In retrospect, it seems odd that the idea of a referendum took such a long time to catch hold. On the face of it, the idea had an enormous amount to offer—to the anti-Marketeers, but also to Wilson and the less committed sections of the party. The advantage to the anti-Marketeers of a referendum was obvious: a chance to prevent Britain from joining the EEC or, if Britain were already a member, of securing its withdrawal. The anti-Marketeers could hardly lose by the holding of a referendum. There was every reason to suppose that it would go their way. If it did, they would have achieved their object and also humiliated the pro-Marketeers; if it did not, they would not be significantly worse off than they would have been anyway. The advantages of a referendum to Wilson and other middle-of-the-roaders on the European issue were equally obvious. A promise to hold a referendum on the Common Market would make it possible for the party to present itself to the electorate as more democratic than the Conservatives; it would enable the party to avoid having to take the ultimate decision on the European issue, which divided it so deeply; and it would buy time, since the party need not come to a final view on the issue, even in the form

---

[6] Kitzinger, *Diplomacy and Persuasion*, p. 296.
[7] *Report of the Seventieth Annual Conference of the Labour Party*, pp. 117-18, 144.

of a recommendation to the electorate, until the very eve of any referendum campaign. It was no accident that, once Labour had adopted the principle of the referendum, Wilson referred to it frequently as "a free vote of the British people." It is precisely on issues that divide the major political parties internally that free votes are most likely to be held in the British House of Commons.

The delay in Labour's coming round to the referendum was probably the result of several factors. For the anti-Marketeers, the referendum, although a good thing, was definitely a second best. The best of all possible outcomes, in their eyes, would be for the party as a whole to commit itself against the Common Market in principle and then for the party to win a general election. Then a Labour Government would withdraw Britain from the Common Market, and there could be no question either of a Labour cabinet's going back on a pledge so categorically worded or of the electorate's voting in a referendum in favor of the Common Market instead of against it. But, although that was the ideal outcome from the point of view of the anti-Europeans, they must have realized by the spring of 1972 that it was an unobtainable outcome. Wilson's refusal overtly to join the anti-Common Market camp, and the behavior of the pro-Europeans, especially in the October 1971 vote, must have made it clear to the anti-Europeans that, if they did capture the party, they would discover that the party they had captured was not worth having. It would have been shorn, probably of its leader, undoubtedly of a large proportion of the men and women who gave it governmental capacity and electoral credibility. So, by the spring of 1972, most of the anti-Europeans were prepared to settle for the best they could get—which, after all, was still pretty good from their point of view.

Harold Wilson was even more reluctant to see the party committed to a referendum, apparent though its advantages must have been to him. For one thing, to opt for a referendum was, to a considerable extent, to abdicate the role of political leader in a parliament-based system. It was to say that the institutions which had made one, and in which one had one's political being, were inadequate to the performance of some large national task. For another, Wilson knew—or at least strongly suspected—that, when all was said and done, withdrawal from the Common Market would be a national disaster. A referendum would have the advantage of shifting the final decision out of the party; but it would have the disadvantage of making British withdrawal from Europe, if not necessarily highly

59

probable, then at least perfectly possible. Wilson cannot have contemplated such a possibility with equanimity.

As so often with Wilson, there was another, more personal reason. The fact was that Wilson, never having contemplated the position in which he found himself by the spring of 1972, had gone on record, again and again, as being opposed in principle to the holding of referenda in Britain. He knew perfectly well that, if he opted for the referendum, all of his old speeches would be quoted back at him. He was quite right. They were.

> I do not recall [that Mr. Wedgwood Benn] suggested a referendum on the matter [the Common Market] . . . but I think most Right Hon. and Hon. Members would regret the idea of government by referendum.

> [Asked on a television program whether, if the polls were going against him, he might not opt for a referendum at the last moment.] The answer to that is "No." I've given my answer many times. . . . I'm not going to trim to win votes on a question like that.

> The Prime Minister [Heath] said that I oppose a referendum and I agree—I have always done so, as he has.[8]

Fortunately for him, Wilson, whatever his other faults, lacked the sin of pride. Having come to believe that the referendum was the best way out of a tight corner for the party, he accepted the idea with good grace, while admitting that it was still "repugnant" to him and that it would be a "fall-back, [a] very poor second best" to the party's renewed demand, made at the same time, for a general election.[9]

The referendum bandwagon, once it began to roll, rolled downhill with astonishing speed. The unthinkable, once thought of, began to be thought of by almost everybody. The task of Tony Benn and those who agreed with him was made easier by the way in which the Conservative party had handled the Common Market issue during the 1970 election campaign. The Conservatives, worried by the electorate's apparent antipathy to the Common Market and fearing divisions within their own ranks, had not come out four-square in favor of Britain's joining Europe but had hedged. The party's election mani-

---

[8] Quoted in *Notes on Current Politics*, no. 18, December 16, 1974, "Labour— Speaking for Themselves" (London: Conservative Research Department, 1974), p. 308. The Conservative party has always made rather a specialty of recording the speeches of leading Labour politicians for use on future occasions.

[9] Quoted in *The Times*, April 17, 1972.

festo had declared that, if the right terms could be negotiated, it would be in Britain's long-term interests to join, but had gone on to say that there were a number of obstacles, including some short-term economic disadvantages. "Only when we negotiate," the manifesto had continued, "will it be possible to determine whether the balance is a fair one, and in the interests of Britain. Our sole commitment is to negotiate: no more, no less."[10] More specifically, Edward Heath, in a speech in Paris on the eve of the 1970 campaign, had said that it would be quite wrong for Britain, or any of the other applicant countries, to enter the Community without "the full-hearted consent of Parliament and people."[11] This last phrase, "full-hearted consent," turned out to be a gift to the anti-Common Market, pro-referendum forces. Not only was it evident by 1972 that the British people were not giving their full-hearted consent to British entry; they seemed positively opposed. Since the Conservative leader had spoken of "full-hearted consent," and since that consent was evidently not forthcoming, opposition to the holding of a referendum on the issue could be made to appear undemocratic, even antidemocratic. This was a difficult argument for those opposed to the holding of a referendum to resist.

Their resistance was further weakened by what was happening in other countries. The Irish constitution provided for the holding of referenda on issues such as Ireland's entry into the EEC. The Norwegian constitution, unwritten like Britain's, contained no such provision. The Danish constitution did contain such a provision, but there was no need for the Danes to activate it, since an overwhelming majority of the Danish Folketing was in favor of entry. Nevertheless, during 1971 both Norway and Denmark, as well as Ireland, decided to hold Common Market referenda.[12] It began to look as though Britain would be the only country whose people would not be directly consulted on the issue. Then, on March 16, 1972, something quite unexpected occurred. Georges Pompidou, the French president, announced that a referendum would be held in France on the enlarge-

[10] *A Better Tomorrow: The Conservative Programme for the Next 5 Years* (London: Conservative party, 1970), p. 28.
[11] For an account of how Heath came to give this pledge, see Philip Goodhart, *Full-Hearted Consent: The Story of the Referendum Campaign—and the Campaign for the Referendum* (London: Davis-Poynter, 1976), p. 25.
[12] Several leading figures in the Labour party opposed to the holding of a referendum have stated privately that the Norwegian and Danish decisions to hold referenda in their countries made it very difficult for them to hold the line. On these other referenda, see Grimond and Neve, *The Referendum*, pp. 65-82 *passim*.

ment of the Community. Pompidou's decision was taken for reasons of domestic French politics, but it provided Tony Benn with his opportunity.[13] Only the day before Pompidou's announcement Labour's National Executive Committee had again turned down the referendum idea; but now Benn, speaking at a Labour gathering in London, declared that at its next meeting he would reopen the whole question. He told his audience: "It [will] be an outrage if the French people are allowed to decide whether they want Britain in the Common Market and the British people are denied the right to say whether they want to join."[14]

On Benn's initiative, on March 22, the National Executive reversed itself. With Wilson, Callaghan, and Roy Jenkins all absent, it voted, by a majority of thirteen to eleven, in favor of the principle of consulting the people. The story was the same in the shadow cabinet. The shadow cabinet needed to decide how the parliamentary party should vote on a pro-referendum motion that had been tabled in the House of Commons by two anti-Market Conservatives, Neil Marten and Enoch Powell. On March 15, the day before Pompidou spoke, the shadow cabinet had rejected the referendum idea; apparently only four votes had been cast in its favor. But a fortnight later, on March 29, this body too reversed itself. Now both the extra-parliamentary Labour party and the party in Parliament were committed to the holding of a referendum or a general election on the Common Market issue. Benn's early seizing of the initiative on the referendum and his tireless lobbying for it thereafter had earned their reward. Benn admitted to *The Times* that in the end President Pompidou had won his battle for him.[15]

The consequences of the shadow cabinet's decision of March 29 were momentous—in the short term and also in the long. In the short term, the decision led directly to the resignation from the shadow cabinet of three of the most prominent pro-Marketeers: Roy Jenkins, the deputy leader of the party, George Thomson, and

---

[13] On Pompidou's decision and the reasons for it, see Kitzinger, *Diplomacy and Persuasion*, p. 391.

[14] *The Times*, March 18, 1972.

[15] Ibid. The referendum bandwagon was given still further forward momentum on March 24, 1972, when the Government announced that periodic "plebiscites" (the word "referendum" was carefully avoided) would be held in Northern Ireland on the future of the border between Northern Ireland and the Irish Republic. The Government's decision was taken for reasons that had to do solely with Northern Ireland, but again it had the effect of making the case for holding a referendum on the Common Market harder to resist. See esp. Goodhart, *Full-Hearted Consent*, pp. 43-44, 46.

Harold Lever.[16] Jenkins, in particular, had had enough. He had watched helplessly as the party had moved, seemingly inexorably, from a strong commitment to the Common Market to something like total opposition. Now, in the space of two weeks, the shadow cabinet, the country's alternative Government, had completely reversed itself on an issue of major constitutional importance, simply, as he saw it, for the purpose of embarrassing the Tory Government on the floor of the House of Commons. In a long letter of resignation, Jenkins maintained that the holding of a referendum would split the Labour party, that referenda would come to be used against the very progressive causes—the abolition of capital punishment, the extension of public ownership, and so on—that the party stood for, and that the referendum was not the sort of issue that should be exploited for short-term partisan advantage:

> This, in my view, is not the way in which an Opposition, recently, and soon again I hope, the Government of this country, should be run. . . . If Government is born out of opportunism it becomes not merely difficult but impossible. . . . This constant shifting of ground I cannot accept.[17]

In one sense, the three resignations were easily accommodated. A new deputy leader was elected (also, as it happened, a pro-European), and the other places in the shadow cabinet were filled by the runners-up in the balloting of the previous autumn. But the resignations, in another sense, were deeply alarming. They were yet another indication—as if another were needed—that the pro-Europeans meant business and that, if the slide from Europe went much further, the party would split wide open. Wilson probably had little sympathy with those who had resigned; not being a man of strong convictions himself, he typically found the strong convictions of others a bit puzzling, even distasteful. But the resignations must have reinforced his determination not to permit the party to come out flatly against EEC membership in principle.

His determination was undoubtedly further reinforced by the letters he received from two pro-Europeans who did not resign. Shirley Williams, one of the most popular of the pro-Marketeers, a

---

[16] George Thomson had been in charge of Britain's EEC negotiations under Harold Wilson (see above, chap. 3, n. 14) and subsequently became one of Britain's first two Common Market commissioners. Harold Lever was one of the few Labour M.P.s conversant with the world of international finance; in March 1974 he became Wilson's chief advisor on financial and economic affairs.

[17] Jenkins's letter of resignation and Wilson's reply to it are printed in full in *The Times* of April 11, 1972.

member of the shadow cabinet and the National Executive, and an almost certain member of any future Labour cabinet, wrote to say that, although she was not resigning now because the referendum was not an issue about which she felt particularly strongly, she would find it impossible to remain in the future if the party reduced its commitment to Europe any further. Roy Hattersley, another rising pro-European, while accepting promotion to a more senior front-bench post, indicated that he, too, would be bound to go if the slide from Europe continued.[18] Although formally the three resignations weakened the pro-Europeans' position in the party leadership, the short-term outcome was in some ways quite satisfactory from their point of view. If all of the pro-Europeans had resigned at once, the party would have been handed over to the left and Wilson's position on the Common Market would have become untenable. As it was, the continued presence of a considerable number of pro-Europeans on Labour's front bench served as a sort of guarantee of Wilson's future good conduct. He could not really afford any more resignations. His leadership could withstand one crisis of confidence; it was doubtful whether it could withstand two.

The long-term effects of the shadow cabinet's referendum decision were, if anything, even more important. Especially since Harold Wilson, however reluctantly, supported it, the shadow cabinet's decision gave a certain legitimacy to the National Executive's own pro-referendum resolution which had been passed only the week before. The Executive proceeded to draft a statement linking the policy of renegotiation described in the last chapter to the policy of consulting the people. The key paragraphs in the statement read:

> If renegotiations are successful, it is the policy of the Labour Party that, in view of the unique importance of the decision, the people should have the right to decide the issue through a General Election or a Consultative Referendum. If these two tests are passed, a successful renegotiation and the expressed approval of the majority of the British people, then we shall be ready to play our full part in developing a new and wider Europe.

> If renegotiations do not succeed, we shall not regard the Treaty obligations as binding on us. We shall then put to the British people the reasons why we find the new terms

---

[18] The two letters are reprinted in *The Times*, April 11, 1972.

unacceptable, and consult them on the advisability of negotiating our withdrawal from the Communities.[19]

The Executive's statement was carried by a two-to-one majority at
the October 1972 annual conference, and, rather surprisingly, Labour's
policy on the referendum hardly changed thereafter. The words just
quoted were carried over verbatim into the party's general policy
statement, Labour's Programme for Britain, in 1973, and were re-
peated, again verbatim, in the February 1974 election manifesto.[20]
What had emerged was that the policy of consulting the people was
the policy that divided the party least. When the possibility of holding a referendum had first been broached, James Callaghan had
observed that it was "a life-raft into which the whole party [might]
one day have to climb."[21] He had been right. Even Roy Jenkins
eventually agreed to climb on board, standing successfully for re-
election to the shadow cabinet in the autumn of 1973.[22]

The Executive's 1972 statement, although it spoke of the people's
right to be consulted, left open the question of whether the consultation should be by means of a general election or a referendum.
Both the National Executive and the party's front bench in Parliament
continued to discuss the question for some time. Most of the pro-
Europeans still wanted to avoid the holding of a referendum if they
possibly could. Largely, of course, this was because they thought
that they might lose it. But they did have conscientious doubts as
well. Most of them, like Roy Jenkins, believed that, if one referendum
were held, then there would be calls for others and that the referendum might become an important weapon in the interests of conservatism. Jenkins and other leading pro-Europeans were believers
in a liberal race-relations and immigration policy; they feared that

---

[19] Report of the Seventy-First Annual Conference of the Labour Party, p. 383;
the National Executive's statement as a whole is reprinted as Appendix 7.

[20] Labour's Programme for Britain (London: Labour party, 1973), p. 41; and
Let Us Work Together—Labour's Way Out of the Crisis, The Labour Party
Manifesto 1974 (London: Labour party, 1974), pp. 6-7.

[21] Kitzinger, Diplomacy and Persuasion, p. 296.

[22] Jenkins was reelected easily, coming near the top of the poll. It was a striking
feature of these years that leading pro-Marketeers did well in elections to posts
in the parliamentary Labour party, even at a time when the parliamentary party
was turning against the Market. The explanation lies partly in the fact that the
pro-Market ranks included some of the most able politicians in the party, and
partly in the fact that, as we saw in Chapter 3, the Common Market issue as a
whole mattered far more to some Labour M.P.s than to others; many Labour
M.P.s who were anti-Market on balance nevertheless had no difficulty in voting
for pro-Marketeers for posts such as the deputy leadership and the shadow
cabinet.

the referendum might be used, for example, as a means of repatriating colored immigrants. They were worried that in practice a referendum would not be just about the issue on the ballot paper; other issues, perhaps extraneous ones, might get caught up in it.[23] They were also worried about the interconnectedness of different elements in government policy; a referendum decision taken in one field of policy might run counter to policy in some other field. But, perhaps most strongly of all, those opposed to the referendum believed that it would contradict a fundamental tenet of the British constitution— that Governments and ministers were ultimately responsible for their actions, and that they were responsible only to their consciences, the House of Commons and the electorate. If referenda became a common practice, political leaders might find themselves having to choose between carrying out policies that they did not believe in— indeed that they believed were contrary to the national interest—and sacrificing their political careers. Politicians might become mere time-servers, running errands for the electorate, constantly passing on to voters the buck of ultimate decision. In the eyes of most pro-Europeans, whatever else a referendum would be, it would be a defeat for the parliamentary system of democracy.[24]

The pro-Europeans thus chose to fight a prolonged rearguard action against the referendum. As late as July 1974, with the Labour party back in power, Roy Jenkins and Shirley Williams argued at a joint meeting of ministers and the National Executive that, if a referendum were held on the Common Market, it would then be hard to resist the case for holding referenda in Scotland and Wales and that, if such referenda were held, given the increasing strength of the Scottish and Welsh nationalists, the result might be the breakup of the United Kingdom.[25] But, at the party's annual conference in the autumn of 1974, held following Labour's victory in the second general election of that year, Jenkins, Williams, and the others who thought like them were overwhelmed. A resolution calling for the holding of a referendum on the Common Market within a year was passed almost without dissent. Edward Short, Jenkins's successor as deputy leader, winding up the debate, refused to commit the Govern-

---

[23] France in 1969 provided a case in point. The French referendum of that year was held ostensibly to provide for a reform of regional government. But it became a plebiscite on the future of President de Gaulle.

[24] On this point, see the anti-referendum speech delivered in the House of Commons by John Mackintosh, a backbench Labour M.P., in March 1975. *Parliamentary Debates* (Hansard), House of Commons, vol. 888, March 11, 1975, col. 416.

[25] The meeting was reported in *The Times* on July 26, 1974.

ment formally but used words that really only made sense on the assumption that a referendum was to be held:

I would like to reaffirm that the people of Britain will decide the issue. They will be asked to decide it by October of next year. We believe that the collective wisdom of the British people will produce the right answer and this Government will abide by the answer. (*Applause.*)[26]

The fact was, although no one seemed to realize it at the time, that the choice between holding a general election on Europe and holding a referendum had always really been a nonchoice—or, more precisely, had always been a choice that would become real only in the most improbable circumstances. Once the party had decided in 1972 that the British people should be given the final decision, and once the party had admitted that the final decision might be made by means of a referendum, the holding of a referendum became almost inevitable if Labour were ever returned to power at a time when the option of Britain's withdrawing from the Common Market was still open. (Obviously, if Labour did not return to power, until, say, 1980 or 1985, the option of withdrawing would long since have been closed.)

The reasons why this should be so are fairly obvious, or at least seem so in retrospect. The main point is that no general election is, or can be, a one-issue affair; all general elections involve the re-election or defeat of an incumbent Government. For a Government to hold a general election is for it to run the risk of losing office. Governments therefore generally hold elections only when they are very confident of victory or when they are required to because the five-year term of a Parliament has expired.[27] This being so, any Government, if it believed it had the choice between holding a

<hr>

[26] *Report of the Seventy-Third Annual Conference of the Labour Party,* London, 1974 (London: Labour party, 1975), p. 258. Short's last phrase—"this Government will abide by the answer"—was important. Everyone knew that the Norwegian Labour Government had recommended a "yes" vote in Norway's Common Market referendum and had declared in advance that it would resign if the vote went the wrong way. It did go the wrong way from the Norwegian Government's point of view, the Government resigned, and the Norwegian Labour party's share of the poll was substantially reduced in a subsequent general election. Britain's Labour leaders were determined not to repeat their Norwegian colleagues' mistakes.

[27] This is not strictly true. The Conservatives went to the country in February 1974 partly because they were confident of victory but mainly because they could not think of anything else to do. See Penniman, ed., *Britain at the Polls,* pp. 20-24.

general election on an issue and holding a referendum, would almost be bound to choose the referendum. Why not? From the point of view of the Government's survival, the referendum would be riskless; the election would not. The general-election option might conceivably be taken up by a Government that was peculiarly confident of victory. Alternatively, it might be taken up by a Government that believed the issue in question to be of supreme importance and also believed that the chances of its being settled in the way that it wanted would be enhanced, even if only slightly, by its holding an election rather than a referendum. But these conditions are unlikely to be fulfilled very often—at least in modern Britain. Few Governments in modern Britain are so confident electorally; few issues are so important.

In the case of the Labour party after 1972, this general consideration was reinforced by several specific ones. Labour's decision to consult the people was taken while the party was in opposition. It was taken in conjunction with another decision, to renegotiate Britain's terms of entry with the other member countries of the EEC. The idea was that, with Labour in power and the renegotiations concluded, the Labour Government would then proceed to decide between an election and a referendum. But politically this simply did not make sense. Quite apart from the fact that a general election would put the life of the Labour Government at risk, it must have seemed improbable, at any time from 1970 onwards, that the members of a future Labour cabinet would be able to agree among themselves on whether the renegotiations had been successful or not. The pro-Marketeers would think they had been, almost whatever the terms; the anti-Marketeers would think they had not been, almost whatever the terms. The split in the party would not have been overcome; it would merely have taken on a new form. In other words, the general-election scenario, although no one seemed to realize it at the time, envisaged the Government's going to the country at a time when it was certain to be very deeply divided. No Government would be likely to do this—especially in Britain in the mid-1970s, when, in addition, any Government seemed almost certain to be governing in the face of considerable economic difficulty. The general-election option was simply not realistic.

The chances of Labour's opting for an election rather than a referendum were even further reduced by the timing of the renegotiation operation. The Labour Government formed in early March 1974 was a minority Government; it depended on the votes of the Liberals and the other smaller parties in the House of Commons and could be defeated at any time.[28] It was generally, and rightly, assumed that another election would have to be held before the end of the year or, at the very latest, early in 1975. But the new negotiations with the other Common Market countries would be bound to last for at least a year, perhaps longer. Thus, continuing to press for the holding of a general election rather than a referendum, as many of the pro-Europeans were still doing in the summer of 1974, amounted to proposing that the renegotiations should be greatly speeded up and/or that the next general election should be considerably delayed, simply for the purpose of causing the election and the completion of the renegotiations to coincide. It was just possible that they could be made to coincide; but it was highly improbable. It would have required a great deal of good luck as well as good management. Of course, it cost the pro-Europeans little to keep open the general-election option; one never knew what might turn up, and they felt that the general case against the referendum was worth stating. But it probably gained them little. Those who were betting on the avoidance of a referendum by the late summer of 1974 were betting on a very dark horse indeed.

By the end of 1974, Labour was in power with an overall parliamentary majority. The renegotiations had begun. The decision to hold a referendum had, in effect, been taken. In the next chapter, we shall examine the course of the renegotiations—or "the so-called renegotiations," as many on the Continent preferred to call them—and their effect upon the Labour party.

---

[28] See Penniman, ed., *Britain at the Polls*, chapter 8.

5
THE SO-CALLED
RENEGOTIATIONS

The Labour party came to power in March 1974 committed to consulting the British people about Europe, and also committed to renegotiating the terms of Britain's entry into the EEC. It was clear from the beginning that the outcome of the consultation might well depend on the outcome of the renegotiations—not necessarily because the outcome of the renegotiations would make any great impression on the British people directly, but because the renegotiations were bound to influence the views of the Labour Government and the Labour party.

Labour had spelled out the main objectives of the renegotiations in *Labour's Programme for Britain* and again in its manifesto for the February 1974 election.[1] The party sought major changes in the Community's Common Agricultural Policy so that low-cost food producers outside Europe could continue to have access to the British market. It sought new and fairer methods of financing the Community's budget. It rejected the idea of a fixed parity for sterling, which seemed to be implicit in the current proposals for a European Economic and Monetary Union. It was concerned that the British Parliament should retain such powers over the British economy as were needed to pursue effective regional, industrial, and fiscal policies. It wished the Community to adopt trade and aid policies designed to benefit not just the former French colonies in Africa but developing countries throughout the world. Finally, it rejected any harmonization of value added tax that would require Britain to tax necessities.

The language in which these demands were couched was very

---

[1] *Labour's Programme for Britain*, p. 41; *Let Us Work Together*, pp. 5-6.

stern—as befitted the mood of the Labour party at the time. The February 1974 election manifesto claimed that entry into the Common Market on the Tories' terms had involved "the imposition of food taxes on top of rising world prices, crippling fresh burdens on our balance of payments, and a draconian curtailment of the power of the British Parliament to settle questions affecting vital British interests." "This is why," the manifesto went on, "a Labour Government will immediately seek a fundamental renegotiation of the terms of entry."[2] The emphasis was meant to be on the word "fundamental."

But, although the party's demands were numerous and its language stern, the fact was that Labour had never spelled out its requirements with any degree of precision. Partly because almost everyone in the party was sensitive to the need to give a future Labour Government some room for maneuver in any negotiations, none of the party's policies, as set out in official party pronouncements, had any figures attached to them. They did not contain any tests by which a detached observer could determine whether or not the party's demands had been met—whether or not the renegotiations had been "successful." It followed that much would depend, as the renegotiations proceeded, on the sympathy or lack of it shown by the other eight members of the Community towards the various British demands, and also on the evolving views of the two most important British figures in the renegotiations, Harold Wilson and James Callaghan. Callaghan, the newly appointed foreign secretary, indicated from the outset that he intended to take personal charge of Britain's relations with the Community.

There is every reason to suppose that Wilson and Callaghan saw eye to eye on Europe. They were both by instinct little Englanders—or, if not that, then certainly "Atlanticists" rather than "Europeans." Like Wilson, Callaghan felt more at home in Washington than on the Continent. Like Wilson, too, Callaghan was still disposed to see Britain as a power with worldwide interests, at least as concerned with the future of Rhodesia and southern Africa as with the Paris-Bonn axis or the creation of a common European energy policy. The two men also had in common a distaste for the extreme views of both the "Euro-fanatics" and the more ardent critics of Britain's entry into the EEC. The great ideas and ideals that others could see at stake in the European controversy escaped Wilson and Callaghan entirely. For them, joining the Common Market was like

---

[2] *Let Us Work Together*, p. 5.

getting up on a Monday morning; it was something one might have to do, but it was not something to get excited about. Their preoccupation, far more than with Europe, was with preserving the unity of the Labour party and with preserving their own positions of leadership within it. A few years before, in 1971, they had been rivals, or at least potential rivals, for the leadership. Now Callaghan seemed to accept that Wilson would remain at the head of the party for the foreseeable future, and the two men worked amicably, and very closely, together.[3]

Probably neither man had a "strategy" with regard to the renegotiations; rather, they had an "approach." Their views were probably remarkably similar to those expressed in the party's official statements. On the one hand, they did want Britain to remain a member of the EEC. On the other, they hated to see Britain humiliated and believed that the terms negotiated by the Heath Government had been humiliating; in or out of the EEC, they wanted to see British interests put first. More than that, both men knew perfectly well that, by appearing to be tough in the renegotiations, they could impress the anti-Europeans and the waverers in the Labour party and at the same time maximize Britain's bargaining position vis-à-vis the other members of the Community. The fact that both Wilson and Callaghan had residual, emotional doubts about Europe undoubtedly increased their effectiveness as negotiators.

In the case of Callaghan, there was another, more personal factor at work. Callaghan is an intuitive politician, somewhat in the style of an old-fashioned American city boss. He is most confident, and most effective, in political situations in which he feels completely at home—where he knows the local people and the local rules of the game. His political antennae in such situations are extraordinarily sensitive. But when Callaghan is among strangers, when he does not feel politically at home, he can be arrogant, aggressive, surly even; his loss of confidence can greatly reduce his effectiveness.[4] So it was with the renegotiations. He began in a style that offended all of the other members of the Community and was the despair of the British Foreign Office. It really did seem at first as though the renegotiations might fail. But gradually he began to take the measure of the new situation—to understand the people, to have a feel for what motivated them. Gradually he became more relaxed and there-

---

[3] See Butler and Kitzinger, *The 1975 Referendum*, p. 45.

[4] The phrase "at home" in the paragraph above should not be taken too literally. For example, Callaghan, having been shadow colonial secretary for much of the 1950s, feels "at home" in English-speaking Africa.

fore more effective. More to the point, as he got to know his fellow politicians of the Community better, as he discovered that he could do business with them, his instinctive hostility to the EEC declined. The other members of the Council of Ministers became "his" people; he no longer had any inclination to walk out on them. Thus, the tone of his first statement to the council, on April 1, 1974, was blunt, even hectoring. "The image of the Community in the United Kingdom," he said, "is not good."[5] But the next time he addressed the council, on June 4, he was much more conciliatory. He set out Britain's renegotiation terms at length, but then concluded: "Let us together put these matters right and, when we do, then the Community will be once again strengthened to play a constructive part in the affairs of Europe and in bringing its influence to bear on the problems of the world."[6] The phrase was "when we do," not "if we do."

The British made an important symbolic gesture at a very early stage, despite the tone of Callaghan's April 1 statement. They let it be known that they would not attempt to renegotiate either the Treaty of Rome or the Treaty of Accession that had taken Britain into the Community. *Labour's Programme for Britain* and the party's 1974 manifesto were silent on the subject, but they could both be taken to imply that "fundamental renegotiation" meant renegotiation of the treaties. Certainly innumerable speakers at Labour party conferences had denounced the treaties:

> We [are] firmly convinced . . . that under the Treaty of Rome and under the subsequent decisions made by the six countries, it will not be possible to develop this country of Britain as a socialist commonwealth.

> We have seen the terms, we have seen the Treaty of Accession and we have seen the Bill which was forced through Parliament, and I say they are completely and utterly unacceptable to us.

---

[5] Callaghan's statement is reprinted in full in *The Times* of April 2, 1974.

[6] *The Times*, June 5, 1974. Callaghan's blunt tone at the April meeting was probably accounted for in part by his desire to impress both the other members of the Community and the Labour party back home with his intention to be a tough bargainer. It has also been suggested that between April and June Callaghan warmed to the Community because he realized that the regular foreign-policy consultations among the Nine might help to halt the decline in Britain's influence in the world. See Butler and Kitzinger, *The 1975 Referendum*, pp. 32-33.

I am, indeed I always have been, opposed to the Treaty of Rome.[7]

But Wilson and Callaghan were well aware that to demand changes in the treaties would be to demand something that could not be obtained. The other members of the Community were simply not prepared to have called into question the entire work of the EEC for the previous seventeen years; in any case, it would almost certainly be impossible in practice to obtain the unanimous consent to any treaty revisions of all of the other eight member countries. Accordingly, although Callaghan continued formally to reserve Britain's right to propose modifications in the treaties, he made it clear that he hoped, and believed, that Britain's requirements could be met within the existing framework.

The term "renegotiations" conjures up a fairly precise image in one's mind: of negotiators sitting round a table hammering out new agreements, with an agreed agenda and a list of demands in front of them. But Britain's renegotiations with the EEC were not quite like that; indeed they were not like that at all. For one thing, the EEC was a developing institution, with a momentum and preoccupations of its own. The other members were not in a mood to stop work on everything they were doing simply in order to accommodate the British. They could not have done so even if they had wanted to; discussions on agricultural prices, for example, went on almost continuously. Equally important, Britain was not some outside body with which the EEC was negotiating; Britain was a member of the EEC and had been for about eighteen months. Britain was represented on all of the main EEC institutions; many of the EEC's officials were British. It was thus not like a trade union negotiating with an employer; it was more like the bargaining among different operating units of a large multinational company. The bargaining went on, but so did the company's business.

As the renegotiations proceeded, many of the items on Labour's renegotiation agenda either were subsumed under corresponding items on the Community's own agenda or were overtaken by events. A few of them turned out to be based on a misunderstanding of what the Community intended. No effort was made to impose on Britain

---

[7] As in the case of the alleged link between the Common Market and capitalism (see above, pp. 48–49), the party conference reports contain a wealth of remarks about the iniquity of, especially, the Treaty of Rome. The ones quoted above were chosen pretty much at random. The specific references are, in order: *Report of the Seventieth Annual Conference of the Labour Party*, p. 137; *Report of the Seventy-First Annual Conference of the Labour Party*, pp. 203 and 204.

a harmonization of value added tax, and, without the British doing anything much about it, the prospects for a European Economic and Monetary Union gradually receded into the middle distance. The widespread fears that the Community's Common Agricultural Policy (CAP) would lead to sharply increased food prices in Britain were largely dissipated by the sharp rise in world food prices; participation in the CAP turned out in the short term to have almost no effect on the British food index, and membership of the Community had the advantage of ensuring supplies of food. Fears that officials from Brussels would constantly be interfering with Britain's regional, industrial and fiscal policies proved equally groundless. On the contrary, when the Community established its new regional fund, it was decided that Britain should be a major beneficiary, second only to Italy. So far as the underdeveloped countries were concerned, the Community turned out to be far more outward looking than the British had imagined. The Lomé Convention, signed in early 1975, for example, offered trade, aid, and technical cooperation to all of the countries of black Africa and to the Commonwealth countries of the Caribbean and the Indian and Pacific oceans. An anti-European junior minister described the agreement in the House of Commons as "historic."[8]

The one item on the renegotiation agenda that might have caused serious difficulties was the size of Britain's contribution to the Community's budget. Not merely the Labour Government, but also the outgoing Conservatives, thought that Britain was paying more than its fair share towards the Community's expenses.[9] And the European Commission was inclined to agree. In a report published at the end of October 1974, the commission calculated that, had the existing

---

[8] This paragraph is based largely on the much fuller account in Butler and Kitzinger, *The 1975 Referendum*, chapter 2. Butler and Kitzinger suggest (pp. 39-40) that Britain's membership probably did have the effect of making the Community more outward looking and more concerned with the Third World than it would have been otherwise.

[9] The writer recalls hearing a radio interview, while the renegotiations were in progress, with Geoffrey Rippon, the Conservative ex-minister who had conducted the original Brussels negotiations. The interviewer grew audibly more and more perplexed as Rippon claimed to be in substantial agreement with every one of the Labour Government's main negotiating objectives. "Do you mean," the interviewer asked finally, "that you support *everything* the Government is trying to achieve in the renegotiations?" "Yes, I do," replied Rippon blandly—though he went on to say that he was not entirely happy with the Government's tactics in the negotiations. It is rare in the British system to find an Opposition spokesman so willing to admit to agreeing with the Government.

budget system been applied in full in 1974, Britain would have made a gross contribution of 22 percent to the Community's budget, while generating only 15.9 percent of the Community's gross domestic product.[10] The trouble was that the basis on which Britain's contribution was calculated could not be revised without some major alteration in the way in which the contributions of all of the member countries were calculated. Britain's claim opened Pandora's box. There was, however, a willingness to help on the part of the Community, and at a summit meeting in Paris in December 1974 it was agreed "to set up as soon as possible a correcting mechanism of general application" which would meet Britain's problem and the problem of any other country similarly placed.[11] At a further summit meeting, in Dublin in mid-March 1975, the precise (very complicated) details of the "correcting mechanism" were agreed upon. At the same summit meeting in Dublin, it was also agreed that New Zealand dairy products could have privileged access to the United Kingdom market until at least 1980. This last was not an important issue so far as the EEC was concerned, but it was an issue that bothered the British—not least Harold Wilson, who claimed to have forty-four relatives in New Zealand.[12]

In the event, the renegotiations proceeded reasonably expeditiously and were concluded reasonably amicably. But it would be wrong to infer that they were never in any danger. Quite apart from the fact that some of their demands were large ones, the British proved themselves extraordinarily difficult to deal with. It took Callaghan some weeks to settle down in his new environment. More important in the long run, Wilson had so constructed his new Government that the ministers dealing directly with Britain's EEC partners were almost exactly evenly divided between pro- and anti-Marketeers. Roy Hattersley, Callaghan's chief lieutenant at the Foreign Office, was pro; but Peter Shore, the secretary of state for trade, was anti. Fred Peart, the minister of agriculture, was quickly won round to the Community's point of view; but Judith Hart, the minister of overseas development, remained firmly opposed to British membership of the EEC even though she played a considerable part

[10] Butler and Kitzinger, *The 1975 Referendum*, p. 38.

[11] Ibid., p. 39.

[12] Ibid., p. 41.

in negotiating the Lomé Convention.[13] The result was friction among the British ministers and anger and frustration among the other eight members of the Community. On one famous occasion, in July 1974, with Callaghan unavoidably absent, the British delegation consisted solely of Hattersley and Shore. What one did, the other assiduously tried to undo.[14] Fortunately, the other members of the Community, despite everything, continued to want to help. They appreciated that some of Britain's problems were real ones; they were sensitive to Wilson's and Callaghan's problems in dealing with the Labour party; above all, they did not want Britain to leave the Community—and knew that, because of the referendum, this outcome was perfectly possible. The process of renegotiation was also facilitated by coincidental changes of political leadership in France and Germany: Giscard d'Estaing, the new French president, was more amenable than his predecessor, Pompidou; Helmut Schmidt, Willy Brandt's successor as German chancellor, was cool and a pragmatist, somewhat in the Wilson-Callaghan style.[15]

With the Dublin summit in March 1975, the formal renegotiations between Britain and the other members of the Community came to an end. It remained for the British Government and the Labour party to decide whether or not they had been a success.

While the renegotiations were still continuing, three very important decisions concerning procedure were taken by the British Government. The first was foreshadowed at the end of the previous chapter. In mid-January 1975, the cabinet at last decided that the British people should indeed be consulted by means of a referendum rather than a general election. Several of the pro-Europeans remained vaguely unhappy about the idea of a referendum, but no one seriously suggested that the Labour Government, having gone to the country as recently as the previous October, should now put its narrow parliamentary majority at risk by going to the country again—certainly not with the referendum option available to it. Immediately following the cabinet's decision, work on detailed plans for the conduct of the referendum was set in train.

---

[13] Despite Judith Hart's opposition to Britain's EEC membership, she was widely credited with playing a constructive part in the negotiations leading up to the Lomé Convention, and indeed with being positive in all of her dealings with the other members of the Community. There was considerable disappointment on the Continent when during the referendum campaign she emerged as a leading figure in the "no" camp. See Butler and Kitzinger, *The 1975 Referendum*, p. 40.

[14] Ibid., pp. 27-28.

[15] Ibid., pp. 31-32.

The second decision attracted less attention than the first but was every bit as important. It was that, when the time came, the Government would formally recommend to the voters whether or not they should accept the new terms being offered to Britain by the Community. Oddly, Labour's official party pronouncements were silent on this point. They said that the people's verdict should be final, but they did not say whether a Labour Government should advise them on what their verdict should be.[16] At first there was some suggestion that the Government should not make a recommendation, that it should remain strictly neutral in any referendum campaign. This view had a certain attraction for the anti-Marketeers in the cabinet, once it was clear that the Government's recommendation, if it made one, would be for staying in. But most members of the Government, whatever their views on the substance of the issue, must have felt that it would be simply absurd for the Government not to make a recommendation. Furthermore, the other members of the EEC were very unhappy about the idea that the British Government, having brought the renegotiations to a conclusion, should then, in effect, wash its hands of them. At all events, Callaghan, as early as his statement of June 4, 1974, was quite categorical: "In submitting the results of the renegotiation to the British people, we shall make clear our verdict on what has been achieved."[17] Later in the year, Wilson declared that, if the renegotiations proved successful, he personally would commend the new terms to the electorate.[18]

The third decision was all but inevitable, although it represented a substantial departure from normal British constitutional practice. It was that, when the Government came finally to make its recommendation to the people, any ministers who dissented from it should be free to voice their dissent publicly, and indeed should be free to campaign actively against the majority view during the referendum period. The normal rule in Britain is that members of a Government, if they are unhappy about a collective decision of the Government, must either keep their unhappiness to themselves or resign. By no means everyone was pleased about the idea of departing from this rule, even temporarily. A few pro-Marketeers, believing that the

<hr>

[16] See *Labour's Programme for Britain*, pp. 40-42; *Let Us Work Together*, pp. 5-7; and *Britain Will Win with Labour*, The Labour Party Manifesto October 1974 (London: Labour party, 1974), p. 26.

[17] *The Times*, June 5, 1974.

[18] *The Times*, December 8, 1974. It is likely that Helmut Schmidt, who visited Britain in late November and early December 1974, put considerable pressure on Wilson to commit himself publicly. See Butler and Kitzinger, *The 1975 Referendum*, p. 37.

Government's recommendation would go their way, wanted to force the anti-Marketeers to toe the line. Quite a few others, including undoubtedly the prime minister, were not greatly enamored of the idea of senior ministers' attacking each other—or at least attacking each other's views—in full view of the public. But it was clear that the choice lay, not between freedom and collective responsibility, but between freedom and the break-up of the Government, since everybody knew that a number of senior ministers—including Peter Shore and possibly Michael Foot—would resign rather than accept the Government's decision if it went against them.

Accordingly, on January 23, 1975, Wilson announced formally the Government's agreement to differ:

> The circumstances of this referendum are unique, and the issue to be decided is one on which strong views have long been held which cross party lines. The Cabinet has therefore decided that if, when the time comes, there are members of the Government (including members of the Cabinet) who do not feel able to accept and support the Government's recommendation, whatever it may be, they will, once the recommendation has been announced, be free to support and speak in favour of a different conclusion in the referendum campaign.[19]

Later, still worried about the possible effects of ministers' new-found freedom, Wilson issued a more elaborate set of rules of conduct:

> This freedom does not extend to parliamentary proceedings and official business. Ministers responsible for European aspects of Government business who themselves differ from the Government's recommendation . . . will state the Government's position and will not be drawn into making points against the Government recommendation. . . . I have asked all ministers to make their contributions to the public campaign in terms of issues, to avoid personalizing or trivializing the argument, and not to allow themselves to appear in direct confrontation, on the same platform or pro-

---

[19] The Times, January 24, 1975. The only precedent for the 1975 agreement to differ was the National Government's 1932 decision to permit open disagreement about whether Britain should retain its traditional policy of free trade or adopt protective tariffs. For a full discussion of the 1932 precedent and its bearing on the events of 1975, see Goodhart, Full-Hearted Consent, pp. 219-26.

gramme, with another minister who takes a different view on the Government recommendation.[20]

It remained to be seen whether in the heat of the battle these admirable rules would be adhered to.

The renegotiations between Britain and the other EEC member states constituted, as it were, the international dimension of the Labour party's internal conflict over Europe. But there remained a domestic dimension; or, to put it another way, while much of the infighting with Labour in power was now taking place in Brussels and Luxembourg, much of it continued to take place in Britain. In forming his Government in early March 1974, Wilson saw to it, not merely that the cabinet was evenly divided on Europe, but also that all of the cabinet committees dealing with Europe were similarly divided.[21] Thus, no decision relating in any way to Europe could be taken without having to run a gauntlet between pro- and anti-Marketeers. The anti-Europeans in the cabinet never tried to challenge directly the basis on which the renegotiations were being conducted; with the prime minister and the foreign secretary both against them, they probably realized that they would lose. But they seized every opportunity to throw obstacles in the way of the negotiations and to make life difficult for their pro-European colleagues. The differences among ministers that were visible to the other members of the Community in Brussels were but a small fraction of the differences that existed. Ministers whose work did not take them into the European field were very glad to be out of it.

For the most part, however, the doctrine of collective responsibility continued to be observed. Very little of what went on behind closed doors in Whitehall was reported in the press. Only the occasional incident revealed how profound the feelings on both sides were. The most spectacular such incident occurred during the October 1974 election campaign. One day Shirley Williams appeared on the

---

[20] *The Times*, April 8, 1975. It was one thing to promulgate the rule about parliamentary business, another to enforce it. Eric Heffer, a left-wing junior minister, was forced to resign for making an anti-Common Market speech in the House of Commons in April; but other anti-European ministers, while being somewhat more circumspect, could nonetheless make it clear, even in Parliament, what their views were. Peter Shore was particularly given to using the Government dispatch box as an anti-Common Market platform. For examples of Shore's dispatch-box tactics, see Goodhart, *Full-Hearted Consent*, pp. 225-26.

[21] On the cabinet, see Penniman, ed., *Britain at the Polls*, pp. 177-78; on the cabinet committees, see Butler and Kitzinger, *The 1975 Referendum*, p. 27, n. 6. The "even division" referred to in the cabinet was three-way: one-third pro-European, one-third anti-European, one-third uncommitted.

platform together with Harold Wilson at one of Labour's regular campaign press conferences. A reporter asked Mrs. Williams what she would do, given that she was a member of a Government committed to accepting the people's verdict on Europe as binding, if the people's verdict was in favor of withdrawal. Wilson, sensing trouble, attempted to field the question himself, maintaining that both of them were on the platform to answer questions about Government and party policy and that Labour was united behind its manifesto. But Mrs. Williams, obviously miffed at being prevented from answering a question that had clearly been addressed to her, refused to be silenced. When the prime minister had done, she responded that it was a fair question and that she proposed to answer it. "Speaking for myself," she said, "I would not remain in active politics if the referendum went the wrong way from my point of view."[22] The next day Roy Jenkins felt constrained to follow suit, announcing that he, too, would resign from the cabinet if the people voted "no."[23] In the event, the episode appears to have had little effect on the campaign or on relations inside the Government; but it was a fair indication of how tough the referendum campaign might turn out to be when the time came.

Meanwhile, whatever the concessions being won by the Government's negotiators in Brussels, the line taken by the Labour party outside Parliament continued to harden. Because of the October election, the party's 1974 annual conference was delayed and was held in London in late November. Although Labour's policy had been set out in *Labour's Programme for Britain* and reiterated in both of the 1974 election manifestos, an emergency resolution was moved at the conference which went far beyond anything the party had said so far. It demanded "complete safeguards" on eight points, including:

the right of the British Parliament to reject any European Economic Community legislation, directives or orders, when they are issued, or at any time after they are issued . . . the

---

[22] *The Times*, September 26, 1974. Mrs. Williams was widely praised for being so forthright. "Mrs. Shirley Williams' political honesty," the *Guardian* said the next day, "shines through this rather shabby election like a good deed in a naughty world."

[23] *The Times*, September 27, 1974. Not many people noticed that Shirley Williams and Roy Jenkins were not saying the same thing. Shirley Williams was saying that, if the referendum went the wrong way from her point of view, she would leave politics; Roy Jenkins was saying only that he would leave the cabinet. Jenkins seems to have wanted to keep open the option of resisting Britain's withdrawal from the EEC in Parliament if, say, the "no" majority was very narrow and/or was registered on a very low poll.

right of the British Parliament to restrict capital inflows and outflows . . . the right of the British Parliament to subsidise food and import food free of duty . . . [and] the right of the British Parliament to control Labour movements into Britain.[24]

As with the similar resolution passed at the 1972 annual conference, it was a case of Labour's being willing to join the European church—provided only that it abandoned its religion.[25] The motion also called for the holding of a special party conference on Europe once the results of the renegotiations were known. The motion was opposed by the deputy leader of the party and even by some anti-Marketeers, who did not wish to see the party even further divided. Even so, it was carried, by 3,007,000 votes to 2,849,000.[26]

But it was up to the cabinet to decide what recommendation to make to the British people. Immediately after the Dublin summit, the cabinet met twice in two days, on March 17 and again on March 18, 1975. It was clear by this time that a majority of ministers would be in favor of the new terms; but it was not clear how large the majority would be. In the end, all but one of those who had been undecided when the Government was first formed in March 1974 came down in favor of continued membership; and so did two ministers who had hitherto been anti, Fred Peart, the minister of agriculture, and Reg Prentice, the minister of education. Peart had been convinced by his experience of negotiating in Brussels that his fears

---

[24] *Report of the Seventy-Third Annual Conference of the Labour Party*, London, 1974 (London: Labour party, 1975), p. 251.

[25] On the 1972 resolution, see above, p. 44 and n. 23.

[26] *Report of the Seventy-Third Annual Conference of the Labour Party*, p. 260. Joe Gormley, a miners' leader, spoke for many in the party, including many anti-Europeans, when he said, in opposing the motion (pp. 255-56): "But what I want to see . . . is to get this damn thing out of the way. For the last seven or eight years we have been destroying ourselves with disunity on this issue. There have been more personalities created and more ill feeling reached by this than by any single topic that we have ever discussed. Is this [motion] telling us that the Common Market is the only thing that socialists should be talking about? I think it is completely stupid. . . . It has split this organisation to smithereens and it will continue to do so that unless we get it out of the way one way or the other." The 1974 conference was also addressed (pp. 315-18) by Helmut Schmidt, the German chancellor, who made a tactful, humorous speech urging the British Labour party not to abandon the cause of European social democracy. With regard to the conference's extreme anti-Common Market resolution, which had been passed only the day before, Schmidt remarked (p. 317): "I cannot totally avoid putting myself in the position of a man who, in front of the ladies and gentlemen belonging to the Salvation Army, tries to convince them of the advantages of drinking. (*Laughter and applause*)."

about the EEC had been unfounded.[27] When the final vote was taken, the tally in the cabinet in favor of Europe was sixteen votes to seven.[28]

The political consequences of the renegotiations were thus momentous. They brought about an improvement in the terms of Britain's EEC membership. Much more important, they made it possible for Wilson and Callaghan to present themselves as reluctant converts to the European cause, they transformed a hitherto evenly divided cabinet into one with a solid pro-European majority, and they made it possible for a Labour Government to join the Conservatives and Liberals in recommending that the British people vote "yes" in the coming referendum. The renegotiations were the result of factional infighting within the Labour party, but in the end they may actually have been a necessary condition of Britain's remaining a member of the EEC.

The factional infighting, however, continued. Ever since 1972, the leadership of the Labour party and the party's rank and file, especially outside Parliament, had been drifting further and further apart on the European issue. The leadership remained loyal to the principle of EEC membership if not always to the practice; the rank and file was increasingly opposed to both principle and practice. Now the leadership, in the form of the cabinet, was recommending that the British people should commit themselves to Europe irrevocably. The reaction of the anti-Market forces in the party was immediate—and explosive.

On March 19, 1975, the day after the cabinet took its decision, Ian Mikardo, a left-wing, anti-European member of the National Executive, tabled a motion calling on the Executive to condemn the results of the renegotiations as falling "very far short of the . . . objectives which have been party policy for more than ten years and were embodied in our last two election manifestos" and to

---

[27] The one minister who had been undecided in March 1974 and now voted against staying in was Eric Varley, the energy minister. Varley was something of a protégé of Harold Wilson, and it was widely thought that, although he was not keen on the Common Market, he would vote in favor of it in the end. No one seemed to know quite why he took the line he did. In the event he played almost no part in the referendum campaign. Fred Peart appears to have been won over not least by the sociability and good fellowship of the Common Market agriculture ministers, who formed, and form, a veritable community within the Community. It is often said that European agriculture ministers from different countries have more in common with each other than they do with their cabinet colleagues in their own countries. On Reg Prentice, see above, p. 36.

[28] For further details, see Butler and Kitzinger, *The 1975 Referendum*, pp. 48-49. The fact that the cabinet voted at all was in itself remarkable. Votes in the British cabinet are very rare; decisions are usually based on "the sense of the meeting."

recommend to the special party conference that Britain should withdraw from the EEC. The motion went further and called on the party as an organization to campaign for withdrawal; that is, the motion called on the Labour party to campaign against the Labour Government. In spite of (or perhaps because of) its extreme language, Mikardo's motion attracted the signature of fully eighteen of the National Executive's twenty-nine members.[29] To make matters worse, on March 22 the Scottish Labour party conference voted by 346,000 votes to 280,000 in favor of withdrawal, and on March 23 five of the seven dissenting members of the cabinet issued a statement opposing the Government's policy.

In the event, Mikardo's motion was never put to the Executive. Its author had clearly overplayed his hand.[30] Instead the NEC approved a memorandum submitted by the party's general secretary, indicating how the party ought to conduct itself during the campaign. "Individuals and individual [constituency] parties," it said, "could not be called upon, still less instructed, to campaign for a point of view contrary to their own individual conviction."[31] This decision was a victory, if a very partial one, for the pro-Europeans; but they soon suffered another setback. On April 9, at the end of a three-day debate in the House of Commons on the Government's recommendation in favor of continued EEC membership, more than half of the Labour M.P.s who voted voted against their own Government; the figures were 137 in favor of the Government's motion, 145 against, with 33 M.P.s on the Labour side either abstaining or paired. Nor was the revolt only a revolt of backbenchers. Of the 62 junior ministers (that is, members of the Government outside the cabinet) who voted, 31 voted in favor of the Government, 31 against, and another 9 abstained or were paired. In other words, not only could the Labour Government not carry its supporters outside Parliament; it could not carry them inside either. The Government's motion was

---

[29] See Butler and Kitzinger, The 1975 Referendum, p. 49. The following account of the infighting in the Labour party is based largely on Butler and Kitzinger, pp. 49-53 and 112-14.

[30] Once again, it was a case of some of the more moderate anti-Marketeers' not wanting to push their pro-Market colleagues too far. It was clear that an active anti-Common Market campaign run by the Labour party organization against the Labour Government would split the party even more deeply than it was already and would embarrass the Government on other issues. Jack Jones, the transport workers' leader, seems to have exercised a moderating influence; see Butler and Kitzinger, The 1975 Referendum, p. 50.

[31] Labour and the Common Market: Report of a Special Conference of the Labour Party, Sobell Sports Centre, Islington, London, 26 April 1975 (London: Labour party, 1975), p. 44.

passed by the House of Commons as a whole—by 398 votes to 172—but only because the Conservatives and Liberals remained true to their European convictions.[32]

There was now not any doubt that, when the special Labour party conference convened, it too would repudiate the Government's position. The conference duly met, at an indoor sports center in London, on April 26. It had before it a National Executive Committee statement stating that the Community's terms, even as renegotiated, did not, in the Executive's view, satisfy Britain's requirements and that the NEC was therefore opposed to continued British membership in the Common Market.[33] The prime minister spoke forcefully in favor of the Government's policy, and so did the foreign secretary. But the conference, as predicted, voted overwhelmingly—by 3,724,000 votes to 1,986,000—against the Government and in favor of the NEC.[34] In the days of maneuvering that followed, the pro-Marketeers were again able to prevent the official party organization from being mobilized against the Government; but the fact remained that, on the eve of a campaign in the country that would inevitably decide Britain's future one way or the other for generations to come, the Labour Government found arrayed against it the Labour party con-

---

[32] The figures quoted above include the two tellers on each side. For a detailed analysis, see David McKie, "On the curious political affiliations and trends thrown up by the voting," *Guardian*, April 11, 1975. No Liberals and only eight Conservatives voted against the Government's motion. Within the Labour party, the votes broke down as follows: members of the cabinet, for 14, against 7, did not vote 0; junior ministers, for 31, against 31, did not vote 9; backbenchers, for 92, against 107, did not vote 24; total, for 137, against 145, did not vote 33. In other words, of the total membership of the parliamentary Labour party of 315, only 137 supported the Government's position (though a few members may have been paired in favor). It seems clear that the Government was not supported even by some M.P.s who secretly intended to vote "yes" on the day. Since the vote was a free vote, it cost such M.P.s nothing to be seen publicly to be siding with the party conference and the majority of party militants.

[33] *Labour and the Common Market*, London, April 1975, p. 43.

[34] Ibid., p. 42. For a detailed analysis of the vote, especially of how the trade unions voted, see Butler and Kitzinger, *The 1975 Referendum*, pp. 112-13. This is not the place to discuss in detail the relationship between the Labour party outside Parliament and the Labour party inside, or between the Labour party organization as a whole and a Labour Government. The main point is that, when a Labour Government is in power, the Labour party outside Parliament can influence the Government but it cannot dictate to it. It was thus perfectly possible in 1975 for the party to be saying one thing and the Government another—possible but highly embarrassing, at least for the Government. The classic study of the distribution of power within the Conservative and Labour parties is R. T. McKenzie, *British Political Parties*, 2d ed. (London: Heinemann, 1963).

ference, a majority of Labour members of Parliament, and a majority of the country's leading trade unions.

Under the circumstances, the mood of the Government at the end of April 1975, and of the pro-European forces generally, might have been one of gloom and foreboding. In fact, it was one of quiet optimism. As we shall see in the next chapter, public opinion, which had for so long appeared so hostile to Europe, had by now swung completely around. On the eve of the referendum campaign, it was the anti-Europeans, not the pro-Europeans, who were beginning to wonder whether the referendum had really, after all, been such a good idea.

6
CONSULTING THE PEOPLE

In Chapter 2 we saw that from 1967 onwards, except for a brief period early in 1973, the balance of public opinion in Britain was opposed to membership in the European Community. At almost every stage, the number of those disapproving of Britain's Common Market membership exceeded the number who were in favor. Sometimes the gap was as little as four or five percentage points; more commonly it was as great as ten or fifteen.[1]

Throughout 1974 and even into the early weeks of 1975, the pattern changed little. As Table 6-1 shows, more people thought Britain had been wrong to join the Common Market than thought it had been right; and more people said they would vote in favor of leaving the Common Market, if they were given a chance to, than said they would vote to stay in. Poll findings similar to those in Table 6-1 were regularly reported in the press, and they formed the basis upon which politicians made their calculations. The pro-Europeans continued to fear the outcome of a referendum and therefore to be opposed to the idea. The anti-Europeans continued to believe that a referendum would go their way and therefore to urge strongly that a referendum be held.[2]

---

[1] See above, Table 2-1.

[2] The anti-Europeans could also point to substantial evidence of pro-referendum feeling in the country. For example, in October 1974 National Opinion Polls found that 56 percent of voters thought that a referendum on the Common Market would be "a good idea," with only 27 percent thinking that it would be "a bad idea"; 17 percent didn't know. Support for the idea varied by partisanship and social class. Conservatives disapproved of it by 45 to 41 percent; Labour voters were in favor by 70 to 14 percent. The business, professional, and managerial classes were against the idea by 49 to 39 percent; manual workers were in favor by 62 to 16 percent. Unfortunately, NOP did not report whether anti-Common Market voters were more in favor of a referendum

Table 6-1

RESPONSES TO QUESTIONS ABOUT BRITISH MEMBERSHIP IN THE COMMON MARKET, JUNE 1973-FEBRUARY 1975
(in percentages)

Q: Do you think that we were right or wrong to join the Common Market?

	Right	Wrong	Don't Know
June 1973	39	44	17
November 1973	34	48	18
July 1974	37	50	13
August 1974	31	53	16
October 1974	34	46	20
January 1975	31	50	19
February 1975	39	45	16

Q: If you could vote tomorrow on whether we should stay in the Common Market or leave it, how would you vote or wouldn't you vote at all?

	Stay In	Leave	Wouldn't Vote	Don't Know
August 1974	30	47	13	11
October 1974	33	41	12	13
January 1975	33	41	12	14

Source: *Gallup Political Index.*

But we also saw in Chapter 2 that "public opinion" as applied to the Common Market issue was really too strong a term. Few British voters knew much about the issue; few cared much about it. Voters seldom mentioned Europe as the most important single problem facing the country, and their opinions on the Common Market, insofar as they had opinions, tended to be highly volatile; a voter who responded "yes" to a survey question about British membership in one week was quite capable of responding "no" to the same question

than pro-Common Market voters, but it is almost certain that they were. See *NOP Political Bulletin*, November 1974, p. 6. The findings in the other opinion polls were similar. It should be added that voters' views on the desirability or otherwise of a referendum had no impact whatever on the actions of the politicians. It was quite clear that few voters felt strongly about the issue and, even if they had, there is no obvious way in which they could have brought their feelings to bear.

only a few weeks later. Many voters took their cues on the issue from the political party that they currently supported, and it seemed probable that those who, on balance, held anti-Common Market opinions were more likely to change their minds or not to vote than those whose view of the Common Market was more favorable. In other words, there had been reason from the beginning to suppose that both the pessimism of the pro-Europeans and the optimism of the anti-Europeans might prove to have been misplaced.

Concrete evidence on this point was available by late 1974, though few appreciated its significance at the time. In its regular monthly survey in October 1974, National Opinion Polls asked not the usual in-or-out question about the Common Market, but a more subtle one. "Since February," the question ran, "the Government has been renegotiating Britain's Common Market terms. Do you think the new Government [that is, the Wilson Government which now had a majority in the House of Commons following the October 1974 general election] should go on renegotiating new terms for Britain; stop the renegotiations and get out of the Common Market now; [or] stay in the Common Market on the present terms?" The results were in striking contrast to the other available opinion-poll findings:

	Percent of Total
Go on renegotiating new terms for Britain	48
Stop the renegotiations and get out of the Common Market now	25
Stay in the Common Market on the present terms	16
Don't know	11

In other words, although more of NOP's respondents wanted Britain to get out than stay in given the existing terms, fully 64 percent either wanted Britain to stay in, even on the existing terms, or else were prepared to envisage continued British membership if satisfactory new terms could be negotiated.[3]

The Gallup Poll was asking a similar question at about the same time and, as Table 6-2 shows, was eliciting a similar response. Asked bluntly whether Britain should stay in the Common Market or leave, a preponderance of Gallup's respondents replied that it should leave; but, asked what their view would be if new terms were negotiated and if the Government thought that it would then be in Britain's best interests to stay in, a majority replied that, in those circum-

---

[3] *NOP Political Bulletin*, November 1974, p. 5.

Table 6-2

RESPONSES TO QUESTION ABOUT HOW RESPONDENT WOULD VOTE IF GOVERNMENT NEGOTIATED NEW TERMS, AUGUST 1974-JANUARY 1975

(in percentages)

Q: If the Government negotiated new terms for Britain's membership of the Common Market and they thought it was in Britain's interests to remain a member, how would you vote then—to stay in or leave it?

	Stay In	Leave	Wouldn't Vote	Don't Know
August 1974	54	24	5	16
October 1974	57	22	7	14
January 1975	53	22	6	19

Source: *Gallup Political Index.*

stances, Britain should stay in. Gallup's question was, to be sure, hypothetical; it hypothesized that the Government would in fact succeed in negotiating new terms and that it would then decide that the new terms were in Britain's best interests. But by late February and early March 1975 both of these hypotheses were rapidly becoming realities. New terms were being successfully negotiated, and it was clear that the Government was going to recommend to the electorate that these terms should be accepted. On February 27, 1975, just ten days before the opening of the final Dublin summit meeting, James Callaghan praised the results of the renegotiations so far and declared that the new EEC budget rules would be "of great benefit to Britain."[4]

The electorate responded at once—and decisively—to the new situation. Between early 1973 and late February 1975, the balance of public opinion was never in favor of Britain's EEC membership; from early March 1975 onwards, it was never against it. In January 1975, the Gallup Poll asked respondents (see Table 6-1): "If you could vote tomorrow on whether we should stay in the Common Market or leave it, how would you vote or wouldn't you vote at all?" In January, 41 percent of Gallup's respondents said they would vote to leave, only 33 percent that they would vote to stay in; another 26 percent said they wouldn't vote or didn't know.[5] In early March (the interviewing was completed on the day the Dublin summit

---

[4] *The Times*, February 28, 1975. On the new budget rules, see above p. 77.

[5] *Gallup Political Index*, February 1975, p. 12.

began), Gallup asked exactly the same question. But this time the figures were nearly reversed. Whereas in January 41 percent said they would vote to pull out, now only 37 percent did so. Whereas in January only 33 percent said they would vote to stay in, now fully 45 percent did so—giving a lead in favor of staying in of eight percentage points. The proportion saying that they wouldn't vote or didn't know fell to 18 percent.[6] The findings reported by the other polls were, if anything, even more striking. Both Louis Harris International and the Opinion Research Centre (ORC) completed surveys on March 9, the day before the opening of the Dublin summit. The two polls asked similar questions, inviting straight yes-or-no answers. Both produced substantial "yes" majorities. Harris, with the "don't know's" excluded, reported a margin in favor of Britain's remaining in the Common Market of sixteen percentage points, ORC a pro-European margin of fully twenty-four.[7] From that moment on, the pro-European campaign never looked back; the anti-European campaign never looked forward.

What had happened to change so many voter's minds in so short a time? An essential part of the answer lies, of course, in the fact that this question, put in this form, is misphrased. It implies that the voters who switched had, sometime before February 1975, made up their minds on the Common Market. But most of them had not; most of them almost certainly had no fixed views on the issue, indeed scarcely any views at all. They were therefore likely to respond to any reasonably powerful stimulus that came along.

The change in the balance of opinion reported by the polls more or less coincided with the Government's final negotiation of the new terms. It might therefore be supposed that the new terms in themselves were the source of the change. But this would be too simple. For one thing, the details of the new terms were far too complicated for most voters to grasp; indeed there were probably not more than two or three hundred people in the entire country who could describe them accurately, even in outline. Moreover, the opinion polls found almost no connection between changes in attitude towards the EEC and knowledge of, or views about, the new terms. For example, in

---

[6] Ibid., March 1975, p. 6.

[7] Louis Harris International, March 12, 1975, LHI/17504, p. 1; Opinion Research Centre, "Britain and the EEC: Second Survey," March 14, 1975, ORC 47803/2, p. 2. The number of those saying "don't know" or "depends on the terms" was 22 percent in the case of Harris, 18 percent (the same as Gallup) in the case of ORC. The volume of polling on Europe, which was rather small in 1974 and the first two months of 1975, increased rapidly from the beginning of March 1975.

April 1975, a little more than a month after the Dublin summit, Louis Harris International asked voters whether they could think of any new terms—or changes in the old terms—that the Government had negotiated. Approximately one in five of the sample knew that Britain's contribution to the EEC budget had been reduced; and about the same number were aware of a change in the Community's Common Agricultural Policy. But fully 56 percent of the sample could not answer the question at all; and, more to the point, those who had switched from the anti- to the pro-European camp—compared with those who had been consistently pro-European—were found to be not more knowledgeable about the new terms but rather less. Of the pro-Common Market "loyalists," 53 percent could name at least one of the new terms; of the switchers, only 46 percent.[8]

The new terms did have an effect, but it was an indirect one. As we saw in Chapter 2, there had always been quite a close connection between many voters' views on Europe and the views of the political party they supported. When a Labour Government was in power and seeking Common Market membership, Labour voters on balance were in favor; Conservative voters were against. When a Conservative Government was in power and negotiating for membership, Conservative voters were in favor; it was now the turn of Labour voters to be against. There was, however, an important difference between 1975 and 1967—when Labour as a Government had last been dealing with the EEC. In 1967, not only was it a Labour Government that was seeking entry into Europe; at that stage the Conservative party's commitment to Europe was less than whole-hearted. Partly for electoral reasons, partly out of a desire to maintain party unity, the Conservatives in 1967 declined to give a clear lead. They voted in favor of Europe in the House of Commons, and Heath's personal commitment remained as strong as ever; but in general the Conservatives did not make much of the issue. At the 1970 general election, as we saw, they merely asked for a mandate to negotiate with the EEC—"no more, no less."[9] By 1975, however, the Conservatives' message on Europe was clear. The party and its leader had taken Britain into Europe; the party and its leader did not want

---

[8] Louis Harris International, "British Attitudes to the EEC: Panel Survey," 47510, p. 30. The findings reported in the text do not, of course, prove conclusively that the terms in themselves made little difference, since the 46 percent of switchers who could name at least one of the new terms could have been disproportionately influenced by their knowledge; but the opinion-poll data, taken as a whole, suggest that this is wildly improbable.

[9] See above, p. 61.

Britain to come out. Conservative voters could of course ignore their party's message if they wanted to; but, unless they held very strong anti-European views, there was no particular reason why they should.[10]

The real element of doubt lay on the Labour side. Labour voters had been overwhelmingly hostile to Britain's EEC membership for more than five years—at least since November 1969. The gap between the proportion of Labour voters approving of British membership and the proportion disapproving was never less than twenty percentage points; at times it reached nearly fifty.[11] In February 1974, at the time of the election at which Labour was returned to power, National Opinion Polls asked voters whether, if the Government could not get satisfactory new terms, Britain should stay in the Common Market or pull out completely. Among Conservatives, nearly twice as many voters thought Britain should stay in (60 percent) as thought it should pull out (38 percent). But, among Labour voters, the ratio was more than three-to-one in the opposite direction; 70 percent of Labour voters were in favor of getting out, only 23 percent in favor of staying in—a difference of fully forty-seven percentage points.[12] This gap narrowed after Labour came to power and entered into the renegotiations; but it did not disappear. As late as early March 1975, little more than a week before the Dublin summit, an Opinion Research Centre survey reported that, whereas there was a pro-Common Market margin among Conservative voters of thirty-seven percentage points, there were still more Labour voters in favor of leaving (45 percent) than in favor of staying in (37 percent).[13]

The question was what effect the Labour Government's pro-Common Market recommendation would have on Labour voters when it finally came. In the event, the recommendation's impact was enormous. It goes a long way towards explaining the shift in opinion

---

[10] There were certainly a considerable number of Conservative anti-Europeans. A number of Conservative M.P.s consistently opposed the European Communities Bill in 1972, and there existed a Conservative anti-European organization, CATOR—Conservatives Against the Treaty of Rome. But all of the evidence indicates that most Conservative voters, like most Labour voters, had no very strong views on the matter and, given a strong lead by their own party, were prepared to follow it. If the Conservative anti-Europeans have generally been neglected in this book, it is partly because there were not many of them and partly because they had little influence either within their own party or on the electorate.

[11] See above, Table 2-3.

[12] *NOP Political Bulletin*, February 1974, p. 17.

[13] *Evening Standard*, March 7, 1975. The interviewing was completed on March 2.

that took place among the electorate as a whole; it provides further evidence for the importance that the "follow the leader" phenomenon had had all along. In its survey held early in March, the Opinion Research Centre had still found an anti-Common Market lead among Labour voters, albeit a relatively small one, of eight percentage points. But by early April, when ORC next published a breakdown by party of voters' views on the Common Market, the position had been transformed. There was still an overwhelming pro-Common Market lead among Conservative voters, but there was also now a substantial pro-Common Market lead among Labour voters. Asked how they would vote if the referendum were held today, 53 percent of intending Labour voters replied that they would vote "yes," only 33 percent that they would vote "no"—a "yes" lead of twenty percentage points.[14] Between early April and the day of the referendum, the size of the pro-European lead among Labour voters fluctuated considerably, but never again could the anti-European forces count on a solid basis of support among Labour voters in the country. It was this shift of support, more than any other single factor, that transformed the prospects for the referendum campaign.

It is interesting to note that Labour voters seem to have taken their cues from the Labour Government and not from the Labour party, which was increasingly committed against the EEC. There appear to have been two related reasons for this. In the first place, most Labour voters were probably incapable of making fine distinctions between the leaders of the Labour party in Parliament and the leaders of the party on the National Executive and in the country; in the eyes of most Labour voters, Labour's parliamentary leaders, notably Wilson and Callaghan, *were* its leaders. They were the only leaders that Labour voters knew; they were the leaders with whom Labour voters identified. If *they* were in favor of the Common Market, then Labour was in favor of the Common Market. And that was that.[15]

But there was a second reason, which, if anything, was even more important. Although most Labour voters were probably not capable of discriminating among the different organs of the party—

---

[14] Ibid., April 18, 1975. The interviewing was completed on April 6.

[15] By the middle of May 1975, according to the Gallup Poll, 41 percent of Labour voters believed that the Labour party was in favor of Britain's staying in Europe and only 18 percent believed that the party wanted Britain to pull out; 33 percent thought, not without reason, that the party was undecided on the issue, and 8 percent had no idea where the party stood. See the *Sunday Telegraph*, May 18, 1975.

the NEC, the PLP, and so on—they were perfectly capable of discriminating among its different leaders. In one of the most revealing single opinion polls published during the referendum, Labour voters were asked which of their party's leaders they regarded as "assets" to the party and which as "not assets"; the proportion responding unfavorably was then subtracted from the proportion responding favorably to give each leader an overall positive or negative rating. Of the eight top places in the list, no fewer than seven went to pro-Europeans. Wilson had a positive rating of 67 percent, Callaghan of 44 percent. By contrast, all of the three Labour leaders at the bottom of the poll (Michael Foot, Peter Shore, and Tony Benn) were anti-Europeans. Foot and Shore's positive ratings were derisory: 6 percent and 1 percent respectively. Benn, even among Labour voters, had a negative rating, of minus 2 percent.[16] For thousands of Labour voters, choosing which way to vote on the Common Market must have been made a good deal easier by the simple fact that the leaders of the party in whom they had confidence were urging them to vote "yes," while the leaders whom they believed to be liabilities to the party were urging them to vote "no."[17]

By mid-March 1975, when the Government announced its formal recommendation in favor of staying in, almost the whole of Britain's top political leadership had lined up on the pro-European side. Margaret Thatcher, who had just been elected leader of the Conservative party, was pro-European, so was Edward Heath, so was William Whitelaw, Thatcher's unsuccessful rival. Most of the leading figures in the Labour cabinet were likewise pro-European, and so was the entire leadership of the Liberal party. Apart from

---

[16] Gallup Poll, *Sunday Telegraph*, May 18, 1975.
[17] This analysis assumes, of course, that the voters in question knew where the various party leaders stood on the Common Market. A survey conducted by Louis Harris International (see below Chap. 6, n. 43) indicated that, as might have been expected, there was a good deal of popular ignorance and misinformation on this score. To take an extreme example, fully 34 percent of voters did not know what Roy Jenkins's views on the Common Market were, even though he had been campaigning in favor of British membership of the EEC for nearly twenty years. All the same, in most cases far more voters were right than were wrong. With regard to Jenkins, for example, although 34 percent did not know where he stood, 39 percent did know, and only 9 percent believed, wrongly, that he was in favor of Britain's pulling out. Conversely, 35 percent did not know where Tony Benn stood, but 32 percent did know, and only 14 percent believed, wrongly, that he was in favor of Britain's staying in. In the case of Harold Wilson, 75 percent of voters believed, correctly, that he wanted Britain to stay in. These percentages refer to all voters rather than to Labour voters only, but there is no reason to suppose that the figures for Labour voters would have been very different.

Foot, Benn, and Shore, the only important political figure in the country who was anti-European was Enoch Powell, and Powell was a man who had as many enemies as friends.[18] If the country had been in an extreme antiestablishment mood, it might have used the occasion of the referendum to repudiate its entire political leadership. Indeed on referendum day itself the Communist *Morning Star* published a cartoon showing a married couple leaving the polling station. The husband was saying to his wife, "That's the first time I've had a chance of voting against Heath, Thorpe and Harold Wilson all in one go."[19] But in the spring of 1975 there was no reason to believe— certainly the opinion polls gave one no reason to believe—that the country was in any such mood.[20]

The Legislative Details. It was against this background, of a massive shift in the balance of public opinion in favor of Europe, that the Government took its final decision to hold a referendum and moved on to consider the various detailed arrangements that needed to be made.

The decision itself posed no problems. By the winter of 1974–1975, for the reasons already given in Chapter 4, Labour was fully committed in practice to holding a referendum rather than a general election; no Government which had just fought an election to secure a precarious majority in the House of Commons was about to put that majority at risk by gratuitously fighting another one. The cabinet took its decision in January 1975, and it was announced by Wilson in the House of Commons at the same time as he announced

---

[18] Powell was an important figure in the sense that he was well known to the general public and in the sense that his speeches and other activities were widely reported; but the opinion polls repeatedly showed that the number of voters disapproving of him and his activities was just about as great as the number who approved. See below, Chap. 7, n. 22.

[19] The cartoon is reproduced in Butler and Kitzinger, *The 1975 Referendum*, p. 265.

[20] This remark may come as a surprise to American (and even British) readers who have read a good deal about the British public's cynicism about British politicians and about the electorate's increasing tendency to turn away from both of the two major political parties. The fact remains, however, that there is no evidence that large numbers of voters are totally alienated either from the British political system as it currently operates or from all of the country's existing political leaders taken together. Many voters, disliking or lacking confidence in the Conservative and Labour parties, have in recent years taken to voting Liberal, or at least to thinking about voting Liberal; but, in the case of the Common Market, the Liberals were, if anything, even more firmly committed in favor of British membership than were the other parties.

the cabinet's famous "agreement to differ" over the Common Market issue.[21]

The details proved a good deal more difficult to sort out, and some of them were not finally settled until the referendum bill completed its passage through the House of Commons in early May. They might have proved even more difficult to settle had it not been for the pro-Europeans' substantial lead in the opinion polls. By May, quite apart from the desire of everyone involved to ensure that the referendum was fair, and seen to be fair, it was clear that the outcome of the referendum was going to depend on the will of the voters and not on any detailed administrative arrangements. The pro-Europeans' lead in the polls had the additional effect of disarming opposition from the Conservatives. The Conservatives remained implacably opposed in principle to the referendum but, since it seemed certain that their side was going to win, their opposition was considerably moderated in practice. They voted against the second and third readings of the referendum bill but otherwise did very little to obstruct its passage. On the last day of debate, the Conservatives' chief spokesman on the bill remarked:

> I must remind the Government of how much they are indebted to the Opposition for the exceedingly reasonable, restrained and sensible way in which they received a Bill which was based on a rather unwelcome dodge and device adapted by the Prime Minister [Wilson] in a moment of difficulty for himself.[22]

Of the large number of issues that had to be settled before the referendum could be held, four were of particular importance. One was whether a simple majority of those who turned out to vote should be decisive one way or the other, or whether the referendum act should stipulate either a minimum turnout figure or a minimum percentage of the total poll that would have to be achieved before the Government could be mandated to withdraw Britain from the European Community. Edward Short had referred in his speech at the 1974 Labour conference to the possibility of the Government's insisting on "a minimum size of poll"; and when the referendum

---

[21] On the agreement to differ, see above, pp. 79-81. The reactions in the House of Commons to Wilson's announcement are described in Goodhart, *Full-Hearted Consent*, pp. 83-86.

[22] John Peyton, quoted in Butler and Kitzinger, *The 1975 Referendum*, p. 67. On the passage of the referendum bill, and on its details generally, see Butler and Kitzinger, *The 1975 Referendum*, chapter 3, and Goodhart, *Full-Hearted Consent*, chapters 6-7.

bill reached its report stage in the House of Commons a backbench Conservative M.P. sought to add a clause providing that the result of the referendum would be null and void if fewer than 60 percent of the eligible electorate turned out to vote or if the majority either way was less than two-thirds.[23] But this issue, although important in theory, was unimportant in practice. Since the British constitution does not provide for the holding of referenda, no referendum—whether on the Common Market or anything else—can be legally binding. Parliament can decide whether or not to hold a referendum in any particular case; it can equally decide whether or not to abide by its result. The issue was not pressed because it was clear to everyone, pro- and anti-Europeans alike, that if the turnout were low or the result very close the final outcome would be decided, not by what was written into the law, but by the balance of political forces on the floor of the House of Commons.[24]

A second issue, which might have proved more contentious, concerned the role of money in the campaign. In the British system, it is not possible to buy television or radio time for political purposes; instead time is provided free by the various broadcasting authorities. British electoral politics in consequence are, by international standards, remarkably cheap. All the same, it is possible to spend a good deal of money in British elections—on everything from bumper stickers and ball-point pens through office staff and travel to full-page advertisements in the Sunday newspapers. On the eve of the referendum campaign, everyone was uneasily aware that the pro-Marketeers, backed by almost every large industrial concern in the country, had far more money to spend than the anti-Marketeers, backed as they were by almost no one except a few trade unions. It was agreed that it would be impossible to impose an upper limit on campaign spending (since there were no candidates to whom the spending could ultimately be traced); but it was also agreed that the government should subsidize, in however modest a way, the

---

[23] For Short's speech, see *Report of the Seventy-Third Annual Conference of the Labour Party*, p. 258. The Conservative M.P.'s efforts are described by Goodhart in *Full-Hearted Consent*, pp. 116-17.

[24] The Government was itself committed to abiding by the result of the referendum, whatever it was; but the Government's majority in the House of Commons was very small and it was always possible that, if the result on June 5 were "no," a substantial number of pro-Europeans would join with the Conservatives and the Liberals to prevent the passage of the legislation that would be necessary to take Britain out. Obviously their moral position would be much stronger if the result were narrow and the turnout low. It was widely believed that Roy Jenkins was quite prepared to lead the fight in the House of Commons against withdrawal.

campaigns of both sides. The anti-Marketeers were happy to fall in with this scheme because they needed the money; the pro-Marketeers fell in with it partly because of the money but chiefly because they were afraid of appearing over-rich, of being accused of "buying" the election. In the end, it was agreed, without too much difficulty, that a modest £125,000 should be contributed to the expenses of each side.[25]

A third issue proved more difficult to settle, though, oddly, it had little to do with the Common Market or even with the outcome of the referendum. It concerned the counting of the ballot papers and, even more important, the basis on which the final results would be announced. The obvious course would have been to follow general-election practice, with the votes counted, and the results announced, separately in each parliamentary constituency. The administrative machinery for such a constituency-by-constituency count was already in existence. But this posed two problems, especially for the pro-Marketeers. The first was that there were known to be a number of pro-European Labour M.P.s who had fallen out, because of Europe, with their local constituency parties. If the result in their constituency went against Europe, they were in serious danger of being ousted by their local party, on the plausible ground that they had not accurately represented their constituents' views on the European issue. The pro-Europeans for this reason wanted the count conducted on almost any basis except a constituency one. The second problem concerned Scotland, Wales and, to a lesser extent, Northern Ireland. Pro-Europeans, but also some anti-Europeans, were frightened by the prospect that England might go one way on the Common Market and Scotland, Wales, or Northern Ireland the other. The Scottish National party was campaigning actively against Britain's EEC membership, and opinion-poll data suggested that Scotland, in particular, might vote "no" to Europe even if the rest of the United Kingdom, and the United Kingdom as a whole, voted "yes."[26] If this happened, it was clear to everyone that the separatist cause in Scotland would be given a powerful fillip. Discussions on

---

[25] See Butler and Kitzinger, The 1975 Referendum, pp. 55, 58-59. The Government also agreed to pay for the printing and distribution of a set of pro- and anti-Common Market pamphlets; see below, p. 122.

[26] For example, in early March a Scottish polling organization, System Three, found 43 percent of Scottish voters wanting Britain to come out of the Common Market and only 34 percent wanting the country to stay in; the "don't knows" numbered 23 percent. See the Glasgow Herald, March 10, 1975. Most subsequent polls showed the pro-Europeans ahead in Scotland but invariably by smaller margins than in the rest of the country.

how the count should be conducted continued for several months, the question being complicated by the fact that any attempt to conduct the entire count nationally would undoubtedly pose serious administrative problems. In the end, a compromise was arrived at, which protected members of Parliament but also made no effort to conceal the results from the different parts of the country. The ballots were to be counted, and the results announced, in England and Wales by county, in Scotland by region. The result in Northern Ireland was to be declared for the province as a whole.[27]

The fourth and final issue excited more passion than any of the others but was certainly no more important. It concerned the wording of the question on the ballot paper. Politicians in Britain, as in other countries, know little about opinion surveys; but the one thing they do know is that seemingly slight differences in the wording of questions can have a considerable effect on the distribution of the answers. Applying this reasoning to the question on the referendum ballot paper, many politicians inferred that some nuance of phrasing might actually determine the outcome of the referendum. Their suspicions were reinforced by the findings of an opinion poll carried out in late January and early February 1975, which did indeed find that some questions elicited much larger pro-European majorities than others.[28] Eventually, however, it seems to have been realized that, after a three-month long campaign, few voters would be likely to arrive at the polling place uncertain about what the real issue was or about how they were going to vote. The wording of the question was finally decided upon quite amicably; the pro-Marketeers, by this time confident of victory, even agreed to append the words "Common Market," universally thought to be "boo" words, to the words "European Community," which were generally supposed to be "hurrah" words. The final question, embodied in the referendum act and printed on the ballot papers, read:

The Government have announced the results of the renegotiation of the United Kingdom's terms of membership of the European Community.
DO YOU THINK THAT THE UNITED KINGDOM SHOULD STAY IN THE EUROPEAN COMMUNITY (THE COMMON MARKET)?

---

[27] A more detailed account of the discussion can be found in Butler and Kitzinger, *The 1975 Referendum*, pp. 55, 63-64.

[28] *NOP Political Bulletin*, March/April 1975, pp. 5-34.

It remained only to settle the referendum date.[29] Delegates to the 1974 Labour party conference had been promised no more than that a final decision would be reached by October 1975;[30] but as time went on and as the renegotiations reached their climax, more and more ministers wanted to get the whole business out of the way as soon as possible. The prime minister mentioned the possibility of a June date in his statement on the referendum in the House of Commons in January, and by early April it was clear that it would be feasible to hold it as early as the first Thursday in June, Thursday being the traditional British day for elections. By mid-April it had been agreed that the Common Market referendum—Britain's first-ever national referendum—would take place on Thursday, June 5.

The Pro-Europeans. If the conduct of the referendum presented a variety of problems to the cabinet and the House of Commons, it also presented problems, equally serious, to those who were going to run the two campaigns—the one for, and the one against, Britain's remaining in Europe. Some of the problems had to do with organization, others with strategy.

Precisely because this was Britain's first-ever national referendum, no one was quite sure how it ought to be fought. It is easy for someone not familiar with the British scene to underestimate the extent to which British politics is party politics. Almost all political organizations in Britain are party organizations; *ad hoc* issue-centered or candidate-centered political organizations are virtually unknown. Or, rather, they are known, but they normally function solely as pressure groups; they seldom participate directly in the electoral process. Parliamentary candidates in Britain are backed by parties; it is the parties that raise money, fight national campaigns and, for example, do business with the broadcasting authorities. Moreover, apart from wartime, there is almost no tradition in Britain of inter-party cooperation. The shifting coalitions, both within and between parties, that mark politics in the United States Congress, for instance,

---

[29] There were a variety of other issues that had to be settled—concerning the allocation of broadcasting time and, for example, whether Britons working abroad should be allowed to vote—and some of these issues aroused strong feelings. But there was never any reason to suppose that the way they were settled would determine the outcome of the referendum one way or the other.

[30] *Report of the Seventy-Third Annual Conference of the Labour Party*, p. 258. The promise was given in the course of Edward Short's speech to conference.

have no real British counterpart. One is either on one side of the party divide or on the other. British politics is "adversary politics."[31]

Yet it was evident to everyone involved that the Common Market referendum could not be fought along partisan lines. Pro- and anti-Europeans were to be found in both of the two major parties; both of the parties, especially the Labour party, were internally divided. It followed that some sort of *ad hoc* organization would be needed. The pattern of British party politics and the form of the referendum itself—with its demand for a straight "yes" or "no" answer—suggested what was required: two umbrella organizations that could function for the purposes of the campaign as single-issue political parties. They could deal with the broadcasting authorities and, if need be, with each other; they could raise money and be the recipients of the government's subsidies; most important, they could coordinate the various campaign activities, which might otherwise become a hopeless jumble. The two required organizations were both in being by January 1975. They were both "entirely self-appointed federations of activists."[32] Fortunately, no rival bodies ever challenged their claim to be the two sides' authentic spokesmen.

The pro-European organization was called Britain in Europe (BIE). It was based on two earlier organizations: the British branch of the European League for Economic Cooperation, a small nonparty propagandist organization; and the much larger British section of the European Movement, which dated back to 1948 and had always been the focal point in Britain for pro-Common Market, European-federalist activities. But Britain in Europe was much less a grouping of organizations than a grouping of people. The membership lists of its various committees read like a roll of the great and the good in British politics and British business. Its president, inevitably, was Roy Jenkins, the staunchest European on the Labour side. Its vice-presidents included Edward Heath, who had only just ceased to be prime minister and leader of the Conservative party; Reginald Maudling, another leading Conservative and a former chancellor of

---

[31] The phrase "adversary politics" is used increasingly in Britain to describe the way in which the two major political parties contend with one another, in and out of Parliament. Adversary politics, it is claimed, prevents the rational discussion of important national questions and causes the major parties to spend too much time trying to undo each other's legislation. See S. E. Finer, ed., *Adversary Politics and Electoral Reform* (London: Anthony Wigram, 1975), especially the Introduction and Part II.

[32] Butler and Kitzinger, *The 1975 Referendum*, p. 68. More detailed accounts of the pro- and anti-European campaign organizations can be found in Butler and Kitzinger, *The 1975 Referendum*, chapters 4-5, and Goodhart, *Full-Hearted Consent*, chapter 8.

the exchequer; Jo Grimond, the former leader of the Liberal party; Cledwyn Hughes, the chairman of the Parliamentary Labour Party; Shirley Williams, by this time a senior Labour cabinet minister; Sir Henry Plumb, president of the National Farmers' Union; and Lord Feather, a former general secretary of the Trades Union Congress.[33] Nor were these just names on a letterhead. Most of Britain in Europe's officers, either directly or through their representatives, played an active part in running the pro-European campaign.

There was no problem about money. On the contrary, as we saw in connection with the question of government subsidies, the pro-Europeans were in danger of being embarrassed by having too much money, not too little. Only six private individuals contributed £100 or more to Britain in Europe, but the number of companies making similar contributions was 363. Five of the largest British companies—Shell, Imperial Chemical Industries, Marks & Spencer, Vickers, and Guest Keen & Nettlefold—each contributed £25,000. Thirty-nine other companies contributed £10,000 or more. By referendum day, Britain in Europe had collected no less than £1,481,583— the largest sum ever amassed in Britain for the purposes of a political campaign. The government's grant of £125,000 constituted a mere 8 percent of the total resources available to BIE.[34] The man placed in charge of spending all this money and of administering the Britain in Europe operation generally was Sir Con O'Neill, a former Foreign Office official who had played a prominent part in the negotiations leading to Britain's entry into the EEC in 1973.

It was not enough, however, simply to set up an umbrella organization, even a well-funded one. Those under the umbrella had to be induced to work together, and some sort of arrangement had to be worked out with those who, for whatever reason, chose to remain outside. The people who were having to cooperate in Britain in Europe had never cooperated before, and there was always the danger that they would find it difficult. There was also the danger that the

---

[33] A full list of Britain in Europe's officers and the memberships of its main committees is set out in Goodhart, *Full-Hearted Consent*, p. 126.

[34] See *Referendum on United Kingdom Membership of the European Community: Accounts of Campaigning Organisations*, Cmnd. 6251 (London: Her Majesty's Stationery Office, 1975), pp. 3-8. The figures are analyzed by Goodhart in *Full-Hearted Consent*, pp. 122-23. In fact, the figures given in the text considerably underestimate the total amount of money available to Britain in Europe. Butler and Kitzinger (*The 1975 Referendum*, pp. 84-85) point out that substantial sums, probably amounting to as much as £400,000, were contributed to Britain in Europe before March 26, 1975, after which all contributions to the two umbrella organizations had to be made public. These contributions are not listed in the White Paper cited at the beginning of this note.

politicians in Britain in Europe, while ostensibly championing the interests of Europe, would in fact be more concerned to champion their own personal or party-political interests.

The two main problems concerned the leaders of the two main parties. If either party had impeccable European credentials, it was the Conservatives. A Conservative Government had first tried to take Britain in in 1961; another Conservative Government had successfully negotiated Britain's entry in 1973; the Conservative parliamentary party was overwhelmingly pro-European in orientation. It would have been only natural if the Conservative leadership had sought to hog the limelight. But in fact they exercised a great deal of self-restraint. The issue of Europe was of paramount importance to them, and they recognized that the outcome of the referendum would be decided not by Conservative voters but by Labour. They therefore conceded that Labour pro-Europeans should dominate the campaign. Their decision was facilitated by circumstances inside their own party. Margaret Thatcher succeeded Edward Heath as Conservative leader in mid-February, and for the time being the leader and the ex-leader wanted to keep out of each other's way. A natural division of labor suggested itself. Thatcher could play herself in as leader, while Heath occupied himself with Europe.[35]

The problem on the Labour side, especially with Wilson and Callaghan, was rather different. It was not how to limit their role in the campaign but how to get them to play a role at all. Having successfully conducted the renegotiations, and having recommended the new terms to the British people, Wilson and Callaghan were now more concerned with preserving the unity of the Labour party than with making sure of victory on June 5. They wanted the pro-Europeans to win, of course; but by March the opinion polls indicated that the pro-Europeans were going to win on their own, without any assistance from anyone else. If the vote in June was "yes," Wilson and Callaghan could claim a good deal of the credit anyway, since it was they who had made a "yes" vote possible. If, however, the vote in June was "no," Wilson and Callaghan preferred to be well out of it, especially since both men had made it clear that they would abide by the result.

Other Labour pro-Europeans similarly preferred to remain de-

---

[35] At least this was the theory; but many of the pro-Europeans believed that, in her heart of hearts, Margaret Thatcher was not all that keen on Europe and that she welcomed an excuse not to have to play a prominent part in the campaign. As the campaign developed, the Conservatives' new leader said all the right things about Europe—but she did not say them very often or very loudly.

tached from Britain in Europe, but for somewhat different reasons. The fact was that Britain in Europe was not to everyone's taste. With its big names, its even bigger budget and its lavish breakfasts at the Dorchester, Britain in Europe looked to some Labour Europeans suspiciously like "Business in Europe." They were repelled by Britain in Europe's grand cars and, even more, by its grand manner.[36] In addition, they detected among some of Britain in Europe's leaders more than a hint of "coalition-mindedness"—of a willingness, perhaps even an eagerness, to submerge the differences between the political parties in the interests of some kind of Government of National Unity, of which they themselves, of course, would be leading members. Fairly or unfairly, Roy Jenkins and some of those closest to him were suspected of covert coalitionism.[37] Some Labour Europeans also had a more prosaic reason for wishing to stand a little apart from Britain in Europe. They were conscious of the Europeans' need to appeal to Labour voters, and they feared that Britain in Europe, with its close ties to business and the Conservative party, might neglect opportunities to win support among leading trade unionists. For whatever reasons, a substantial number of Labour's pro-Europeans concentrated their activities on the "Labour Campaign for Britain in Europe," which was launched, with the support of eighty-eight Labour M.P.s, in early April.[38]

---

[36] Butler and Kitzinger refer to the Dorchester breakfasts (*The 1975 Referendum*, p. 71, n. 6). Britain in Europe's air of grandness was sometimes almost breathtaking. Its press conferences were held at the Waldorf Hotel in the Aldwych. One could tell that a Britain in Europe press conference was proceeding inside from the fact that outside were parked the sorts of cars that are normally only seen lined up outside the residences of foreign ambassadors. The style was certainly more a Conservative than a Labour style.

[37] It would have been surprising if men like Jenkins and Heath had not occasionally considered taking part in some sort of all-party or non-party Government. Jenkins believed that the Labour party was moving further and further to the left; he must have sensed that his chances of becoming the party's leader were remote. Heath had just been disowned by his own party, in favor of a former subordinate of his for whom he had little respect. A lot of politicians felt, though few said it publicly, that the party battle in its existing form was preventing the adoption of pragmatic solutions to the country's economic problems. The gulf, especially in the Labour party, between those who under some circumstances would consider joining a coalition and those who would not was a very deep one.

[38] The supporters of the Labour Campaign for Britain in Europe had an additional motive. The launching of the campaign coincided with the holding of the Labour party's special conference on the Common Market (see above, pp. 86-87). In other words, the campaign was launched at a time when there was a real fear that trade unions, trade union branches, and constituency Labour parties might be mobilized on the "no" side. One of the aims of the Labour Campaign was to neutralize such organizations—to make it impossible for the

Table 6-3

REASONS FOR BRITAIN'S STAYING IN OR PULLING OUT
OF THE COMMON MARKET
(in percentages)

Responses	All Respondents
Reasons for Staying In	
Can't go it alone/can't survive as an island	24
Bigger markets/more trade and export opportunities	17
Because we are in now	17
Economic advantages of being part of bigger unit/ group of countries	16
Fewer barriers to trade/more accessible markets	9
Do better together than individually	9
Reasons for Pulling Out	
Prices of everything would be lower/go down	14
We were better off before	12
Independence	11

Note: The question was open-ended. All responses offered by more than 9 percent of respondents are listed above. Respondents could offer more than one reason for Britain's staying in or pulling out.
Source: Louis Harris International, "British Attitudes to the EEC: Panel Survey," 47510, pp. 18-19.

There might have been a good deal of friction between the Labour and Conservative leaders inside Britain in Europe, or between Britain in Europe and Wilson and Callaghan, or between Britain in Europe and the Labour campaign. But in fact there was almost none. Almost everyone recognized the overriding need to win on June 5; almost everyone accepted Britain in Europe's central coordinating role; personal relations remained good. Perhaps most important, it always looked as though the pro-Europeans were going to win. The pro-Europeans were like surfers on the crest of a wave. They could afford to operate independently of one another; they could even afford a certain amount of jostling. Almost whatever they did, the wave would carry them forward.

---

anti-Europeans to claim that they and they alone were speaking for "the party." Britain in Europe, being an explicitly non-party organization, could not do this. The Labour Campaign's efforts seem to have been quite successful, though in any case most Labour grass-roots organizations were content to remain neutral on the issue: they were weary of the party's internal bickering on the Common Market, and anyway it looked as though the "yes" forces were going to win.

From the middle of March onwards, the pro-Europeans were supremely confident of victory. They were, however, never complacent. The risks were too great for that—the risk of Britain's having to leave the European Community, the risk of the economic collapse that might follow, the risk of the power that a "no" vote might place in the hands of the leaders on the anti-European side, Benn, Foot, Shore, and possibly Powell. Since the left wing of the Labour party was the only cohesive political force campaigning against Europe, it seemed almost inevitable that, if by any chance the vote on June 5 did go the wrong way, the left would be among the chief beneficiaries. At the very least, the left's claim to be the true representatives of "the people," which until now never seemed remotely plausible, would suddenly gain credibility. The pro-Europeans could not hope to gain much from the referendum; after all, Britain was a member of the Common Market already. But they had—or felt that they had—a very great deal to lose.

And there was at least one potential weakness in the pro-Europeans' position. Although world food prices were by now, if anything, slightly higher than EEC food prices, considerable numbers of voters nevertheless still believed, as Table 6-3 shows, that prices, especially food prices, would fall if Britain pulled out. Thus, while voters' reasons for wanting Britain to stay in remained diffuse, their reasons for wanting Britain to pull out remained disconcertingly specific. Well on in the campaign, in mid-May, Louis Harris International asked voters who were planning to vote "yes" whether there was any one point being made by the anti-Marketeers that led them to wonder whether they were right to be in favor of continued British membership. Fully 10 percent of the sample mentioned high prices in general (6 percent) or higher food prices in particular (4 percent). Only one other reason—"losing our independence/freedom/self-rule/sovereignty"—was mentioned by as many as 5 percent of the sample. When, by contrast, those intending to vote "no" were asked whether there was any one point being made by the pro-Marketeers that particularly impressed them, no single subject was mentioned by more than 4 percent of the sample.[39] On the basis of this and other evidence, the leaders of Britain in Europe were well aware that prices could prove to be their Achilles' heel.

[39] Louis Harris International, "First 'State of the Battle' Survey," May 23, 1975, 47516, pp. 10-11. Britain in Europe mounted an elaborate program of public opinion polling and made extensive use of its findings. Humphrey Taylor, who was in charge of the polling for Louis Harris International, was a member of Britain in Europe's executive committee.

The Anti-Europeans. Britain in Europe's headquarters occupied some two dozen offices in a comfortable building in Old Park Lane, not far from the Dorchester Hotel. The headquarters of the National Referendum Campaign (NRC) occupied two rooms on the fourth floor of a much less comfortable office building off the Strand. The National Referendum Campaign, despite its noncommittal name, was the umbrella organization of the anti-Europeans. It sought to coordinate the activities of a whole host of anti-Common Market organizations, with names like Get Britain Out, the Common Market Safeguards Committee, the Anti-Common Market League, the Anti-Dear Food Campaign, and British Business for World Markets. Its chairman was, somewhat surprisingly, a middle-of-the-roader, a moderate Conservative M.P. named Neil Marten, whose motion in the House of Commons calling for a referendum on the Common Market had precipitated the Labour shadow cabinet's decision in favor of a referendum before the change of Government.[40]

If the pro-Europeans were like surfers on the crest of a wave, those running the National Referendum Campaign were like swimmers about to be dragged out to sea by a powerful undertow. They could, and did, struggle, and some of them, against all the evidence, remained optimistic to the end; but they had few resources and the forces arrayed against them were exceedingly powerful.

The National Referendum Campaign, for one thing, had very little money. Indeed there is something rather pathetic about the section relating to the NRC in the accounts of the campaign organizations published by the government after the referendum was over.[41] Britain in Europe's accounts cover no fewer than fourteen printed pages; the NRC's cover only three. Britain in Europe's accounts list the names of 369 individuals and organizations as having donated £100 or more to Britain in Europe's funds; the NRC's list precisely 7. Britain in Europe collected altogether £996,508 in contributions, apart from the government subsidy; the National Referendum Campaign collected £8,610. Whereas the government's grant of £125,000 constituted 8 percent of Britain in Europe's total income, it constituted 94 percent of the NRC's. This shortage of money was not only a problem in itself for the anti-Europeans; it drew attention to the narrowness of their basis of support. If, as the anti-Europeans claimed, continued membership in the Common Market was going to prove economically disastrous for Britain, it seemed a little surpris-

---

[40] See above, p. 79.

[41] See *Accounts of Campaigning Organisations*, Cmnd. 6251, especially pp. 18-20.

ing that so few British businesses, or even trade unions, were prepared to contribute financially towards averting the disaster.[42]

All the same, the NRC's shortage of funds need not have proved fatal. The newspapers, whatever the pro-European bias of their editorials, were bound to publicize the anti-Europeans' more important pronouncements, and the broadcasting authorities were required by law to report fairly and impartially the campaign activities of the two sides. Moreover, both sides, as in a normal British election, were allocated an equal amount of free time on television for the presentation of their views.

The anti-Europeans' real problems lay elsewhere, especially in the size and character of their leadership. With almost every senior politician in the country enlisted on the pro-European side, the anti-Europeans could call on only a very limited number of nationally known spokesmen. Enoch Powell, Tony Benn, Barbara Castle, and Michael Foot were familiar faces among the politicians, and Jack Jones and Hugh Scanlon, both ardent anti-Europeans, were well-known trade unionists. But that was about it. As a result, the same few people had to appear night after night on television, and the speakers at anti-Common Market rallies were often wholly obscure trade union officials and little-known backbench M.P.s. Moreover, the anti-European leaders, even those who were well known, were not at all popular with the electorate; several of them were about as popular as Richard Nixon would have been if he had sought reelection in the United States in 1976. Dislike of Benn, Foot, and Peter Shore, as we saw, probably had a good deal to do with bringing many Labour voters into the pro-European camp early in the campaign; and, if Labour voters disliked them, they were even more unpopular among Conservatives and Liberals.

Further evidence of the anti-Europeans' unpopularity was provided by a survey conducted for Britain in Europe by Louis Harris International. A sample of voters were asked to say whether they respected and liked, or alternatively disliked and distrusted, each of twenty-eight prominent public figures, associated with all three major political parties. Of the twenty-eight, seventeen were familiar to

---

[42] The NRC's accounts, taken by themselves, are a little misleading, since one or two trade unions seconded staff to the NRC for the duration of the campaign. For example, the anti-European Association of Scientific, Technical and Managerial Staffs lent its director of research. All the same, the lack of generosity of the anti-European trade unions is striking. The giant Transport and General Workers' Union lent a member of its staff but contributed only £1,377 in cash. See Butler and Kitzinger, *The 1975 Referendum*, pp. 102 and 107, and *Accounts of the Campaigning Organisations*, Cmnd. 6251, p. 19.

more than 70 percent of the sample. Among these seventeen, there was an absolutely perfect correlation between views on the Common Market and standing with the public. The ten pro-Marketeers were the ten most popular figures among the seventeen; the seven anti-Marketeers were the seven least popular. Each of the ten pro-Marketeers had a positive rating (in the sense that more people liked than disliked him or her); each of the anti-Marketeers save one, Enoch Powell, had a negative rating. Even the National Referendum Campaign's own research suggested that, while Enoch Powell might just possibly be an asset to the anti-Marketeers' campaign, Tony Benn was a positive liability.[43]

Not only were most of the leading anti-Europeans unpopular individually; they were very disparate as a group. Neil Marten was almost the only moderate among them. Benn, Castle, Foot, and, to a lesser extent, Shore were all well to the left of the Labour party; so were the trade unionists, Jones and Scanlon. By contrast, Powell and several of the Conservative anti-Europeans were extreme right-wingers; Powell in particular was famous for his attacks on colored immigration and his ultraconservative economic views. This division within the anti-European camp did not prevent its various leaders from working together reasonably amicably during the campaign, but it did prevent some of them from appearing together (only at the very end of the campaign could Benn be persuaded to appear on the same platform with Powell) and, more important, it enabled the pro-Europeans to brand the anti-Europeans as political extremists—an unholy alliance of extreme left and extreme right against the

---

[43] The Louis Harris International research is reported in "The Public Standing of Individuals and Institutions Engaged in the EEC Referendum Campaign," LHI/47509, April 1975, p. 6. The seventeen individuals and their ratings were: Jeremy Thorpe, +29; Roy Jenkins, +25; Shirley Williams, +25; William Whitelaw, +23; Edward Heath, +21; James Callaghan, +20; Harold Wilson, +19; Lord Feather, +18; Lord George-Brown, +12; Reginald Maudling, +12; Enoch Powell, +2; Jack Jones, −5; Clive Jenkins, −7; Michael Foot, −9; Tony Benn, −15; Hugh Scanlon, −17; and Iain Paisley, −59. Readers will note that the most popular anti-European, Enoch Powell, was still a good deal less popular than the least popular pro-Europeans, Lord George-Brown and Reginald Maudling. The analysis in the text suggests that liking and respecting leaders led to views on Europe rather than the other way round. Undoubtedly some voters thought better of individual leaders because of their stand on Europe, but it is doubtful whether this was a widespread phenomenon. The individuals were much more salient to most voters than either their views on Europe or the issue of Europe itself. In addition, attitudes towards the individuals were much more stable than attitudes towards Europe. For the results of the National Referendum Campaign poll, see Butler and Kitzinger, The 1975 Referendum, p. 257.

moderate center. There can be little doubt but that this charge was well founded—and that it stuck.

The other serious problem confronting the anti-Europeans was their lack of an issue. The connection between Britain's Common Market membership and rising prices seemed the obvious choice. The trouble was that the prices issue, as an issue, seemed already to have done its work; there seemed little future in it. People were conscious of rising prices; they disliked rising prices; some of them blamed the Common Market for rising prices.[44] Yet the same opinion polls that bore witness to people's dislike of rising prices also bore witness to their intention to vote "yes" on June 5. It was not at all clear how people could be made more conscious of rising prices than they already were, or how more of them than already did could be induced to blame rising prices on the Common Market. Furthermore, the members of the Government on the anti-European side were inhibited from making too much of the prices issue by their knowledge that the EEC was not in fact responsible for the current price rises in Britain and also by the fact that too much emphasis on inflation would rebound to the discredit of the Government of which, after all, they were still members. If the issue of prices was the pro-Europeans' Achilles' heel, it was going to take an exceedingly lucky arrow to hit it.

The other issue that the anti-Europeans would obviously want to take up was that of "sovereignty"—the issue of the loss of independence that Britain would suffer by remaining an EEC member. This was the issue that Douglas Jay had raised when he had first called for a referendum on the Common Market five years before; it was linked in the minds of many to the retention, indeed the re-forging, of Britain's links with the Commonwealth. That the issue of sovereignty did resonate in the minds of at least some voters is

---

[44] If more people had blamed the Common Market for rising prices, the outcome of the referendum might possibly have been different. After all, in the days when the Common Market had been unpopular, the belief that it led to higher prices had been a major contributory cause of its unpopularity (see above, p. 40). Even then, however, only a minority of voters supposed that the Common Market was uniquely responsible for inflation, and by the time of the referendum campaign factors other than the Common Market loomed much larger in most voters' minds. For example, in the week before polling day the Opinion Research Centre asked respondents which two of a number of factors they thought had been mainly to blame for the increases of prices in the shops. The Common Market (mentioned by 19 percent) finished third, well behind worldwide price rises (64 percent) and the trade unions (47 percent). Predictably, respondents intending to vote "no" were much more likely to mention the Common Market (45 percent) than respondents who intended to vote "yes" (8 percent). See the *Evening Standard*, June 5, 1975.

suggested by Table 6-3; when voters were asked what they thought were the best reasons for Britain's pulling out of the Common Market, some 15 percent of the responses referred to such matters as "affirming traditional links with the Commonwealth," "independence," and "being dictated to by other countries." And the sovereignty issue, after prices, was the one that seemed most perturbing to voters who were intending to vote "yes."[45] But, again, the sovereignty issue, like the prices issue, seemed to have done its work already. If voters did not already realize that Britain's Common Market membership involved a substantial loss of sovereignty, it was not clear how at this late date the point could be brought home to them. It also appeared to be the case that, although some voters were greatly moved by the question of sovereignty, most were not moved by it at all. It was an issue of intense interest to only a small minority, and that minority was already mobilized on the anti-European side.

Perhaps most important of all, the anti-Marketeers had to contend with the general feeling that Britain was already a member of the Common Market, that it would be risky to pull out, that Britain was a small country that could not go it alone, and that it was advantageous economically for Britain to be part of a larger industrial and trading unit. It was not as though Britain had been doing well economically outside the Common Market and had only begun to decline after becoming a member. On the contrary, in the British case, unlike the Norwegian, the Common Market seemed to offer one of the few hopes that there were of the country's becoming economically strong again. As Table 6-3 shows, the feeling was very widespread that Britain's only possible future lay in Europe and that Britain simply "couldn't survive as an island." The voters' caution and conservatism had once worked in favor of the opponents of Britain's entry into the EEC; now it worked in favor of the opponents of pulling out. And, once again, it was not at all clear what the anti-Europeans could say that would dispel this general feeling, which, if it was diffuse, was also by this time tinged with considerable popular anxiety. As the campaign gathered momentum after the Dublin summit, all that the anti-Europeans could do was to state and restate their arguments and hope that somehow, in some way, what they said would sink in.

The Campaign. The referendum campaign itself, though it had an end, did not really have a beginning or a middle. In one sense, it

---

[45] Louis Harris International, "Public Attitudes to the EEC: Panel Survey," 47510, p. 19. See above, p. 137.

had been going on for fourteen years, ever since Harold Macmillan had first announced in the summer of 1961 that Britain was seeking EEC membership. In another, it did not begin until the middle of May 1975, when Britain in Europe and the National Referendum Campaign began their series of daily rallies and press conferences. Either way, by the late spring of 1975 the arguments of both sides were well known and so were most of the personalities. It remained to be seen whether some speech, or some incident, could forestall the triumph of the pro-Europeans, which by now seemed all but inevitable.

Britain in Europe's strategy was straightforward. It was to present the pro-Europeans as moderate, disinterested, above party, representative of all sections of the community. Each evening during the campaign a Britain in Europe public meeting somewhere in the country was addressed by speakers from each of the three main parties. Scores of subsidiary organizations were established, with names like Scotland in Europe, Wales in Europe, Humberside in Europe, Richmond in Europe, Christians for Europe, Actors and Actresses for Europe, even, improbably, Communists for Europe. Much use was made in Britain in Europe's propaganda of stars from show business and the world of sports. Britain in Europe's television broadcasts were produced by an American, Charles Guggenheim, who had made films for George McGovern's 1972 presidential campaign in the United States and whose ciné-vérité style consorted well with the pro-Europeans' desire to present themselves as ordinary people addressing ordinary people. In private Britain in Europe was somewhat grand; in public it sought the common touch. Thus, Shirley Williams was seen on television talking to shoppers, Roy Jenkins in his constituency office, David Steel, later to be the Liberal leader, in a crowded pub. One of the television programs was given over almost entirely to unrehearsed exchanges in a working men's club between Lord Feather, the retired trade union leader, and South Wales steelworkers. Those present were encouraged to voice their doubts about the Common Market so that Feather could reply to them. With his avuncular manner, winning smile, and Yorkshire accent, Feather conveyed to the viewer the sense that the pro-Europeans were Very Important People who were nevertheless in touch with the common man.[46]

---

[46] On the pro-Europeans' use of television, see Butler and Kitzinger, *The 1975 Referendum*, pp. 89, 198-200. Britain in Europe's polling confirmed that its

At the same time, Britain in Europe attempted to insinuate into people's minds the notion that a vote against the Common Market was a vote in favor of extremists, cranks, and other dangerous elements. A cartoon in the London *Evening Standard* portrayed a Get Britain Out march, with Shore, Benn, Mikardo, Powell, and Foot in the lead followed by a weird assortment of bearded Scottish nationalists, anarchists and Communists, long-haired Trotskyists and Maoists, and a solitary goose-stepping, monocled figure wearing a swastika armband.[47] The official spokesmen for Britain in Europe were never so crude; they feared a possible backlash, and anyway leaders among the anti-Marketeers were the cabinet colleagues of some of them. But Edward Heath in Trafalgar Square on March 4 drew attention to the Communist party's zeal to take Britain out of the Community, and Roy Jenkins evoked the same theme at the final Britain in Europe meeting on June 2. For Britain to leave the Common Market, he said, would be for the country to go into "an old people's home for fading nations . . . I do not think it would be a very comfortable old people's home." And, he added, "I do not like the look of some of the prospective wardens."[48]

The dominant figures in the pro-European campaign were undoubtedly Roy Jenkins and Edward Heath. They appeared regularly at Britain in Europe's press conferences, they stumped the country, they both made major appearances in Britain in Europe's television broadcasts. Jenkins argued the European case with passion, elegance, and, most of the time, considerable good humor. The cause was one he believed in, and he relished being able to speak his mind without having to worry too much about the reactions of Labour's left or of the party's more cautious official leadership. Heath similarly seemed released—as though the loss of the Conservative leadership had relaxed him and, paradoxically, increased his confidence. While Jenkins laid stress on the international aspects of the European case, Heath struck a more explicitly patriotic note:

One of the sadder aspects of the campaign is the way the anti-Marketeers are talking Britain down. They tell us that the British people are too weak to hold their own in the European Community, that we are not able to compete in

approach was making a favorable impression on television viewers. On the referendum campaign generally, see Butler and Kitzinger, *The 1975 Referendum*, chapters 4, 5, 7, and 8, and Goodhart, *Full-Hearted Consent*, chapter 10.

[47] *Evening Standard*, March 24, 1975.

[48] Butler and Kitzinger, *The 1975 Referendum*, p. 183.

the open markets of Europe and that we cannot survive the rigours of fair competition. I reject totally that kind of defeatist talk. They may have lost faith but I have not.[49]

The enthusiasm that greeted Heath as he toured the country must have helped to heal the wounds inflicted by his recent defeat. It certainly added a touch of heightened emotion to a campaign that already had the hallmarks of a crusade. As one of the campaigners, someone who had not been terribly enthusiastic about Europe in the early days, remarked on the eve of poll, "I never thought that I would care so much."[50]

Wilson and Callaghan began by holding themselves somewhat aloof from the campaign. Others could conquer Jerusalem; they would spend their time attending to the affairs of their diocese. But Wilson in particular was increasingly irritated by the attacks being made on his Government's good faith and on the new terms that had been negotiated. Towards the end, both he and Callaghan gradually came to play a considerable part on the pro-European side, though a much smaller one than might have been indicated by their positions. Neither would appear on Britain in Europe platforms, but Wilson addressed a number of trade union meetings on Europe and Callaghan eventually agreed to appear in a Britain in Europe television broadcast, though in a manner designed to draw attention to his relative detachment from the umbrella organization. Both men were at pains to rebut some of the more extravagant claims made by the anti-Marketeers, and Wilson in particular sought to emphasize the momentousness of the issue. As he put it in Cardiff on June 4:

Tomorrow is the decisive day in the affairs of our people. When all the arguments have died down and this campaign comes to an end and when the dust has finally settled, tomorrow's decision will be seen not just as a vote, but as a vote about the future of our young people, our children and those who come after them.[51]

---

[49] Ibid.

[50] Quoted in Goodhart, *Full-Hearted Consent*, p. 180. Goodhart remarks (p. 179): "For twenty-five years Ted Heath had been used to applause, but in the past he had always occupied a senior position in the Government or in his Party, and it had been arguable that the acclaim he received was an acknowledgement of the official position he held. But now he had no position, and for the first time it was clear that the standing ovations he received were a measure of the affection and respect in which he was held as an individual."

[51] *The Times*, June 5, 1975.

The anti-Europeans did not really have a strategy; nor could they have, given the profound divisions within their ranks. However great the divisions on other issues between Roy Jenkins and Edward Heath—or between, say, Shirley Williams and Margaret Thatcher— they were as nothing compared with the divisions that separated a Tony Benn from an Enoch Powell. The remarkable thing about the anti-European campaign was not that it lacked coherence, which it did, but that it managed to cohere at all. Its success in functioning as a single campaign right up to the end was due partly to the dedicated but emollient personality of Neil Marten, partly to the passion that the anti-European cause was able to arouse, and partly to everyone's sense that they might as well work together amicably during the campaign since there was no real prospect of their having to work together afterwards. On the anti-European side, as on the pro-European, the essentially temporary nature of the whole affair promoted feelings of good fellowship.

Several of the anti-Europeans—notably Tony Benn, Michael Foot, and Jack Jones—would undoubtedly have liked to campaign against the Common Market on the basis that it was the product of a capitalist conspiracy—that if Britain remained a member of the EEC there would be no real prospect of Britain's ever becoming a socialist society. But they were not in a position to deploy this argument. On the one hand, they knew that it would break up the National Referendum Campaign organization, since the Conservatives and the other right-wingers on the NRC's national executive would not stand for it. On the other, they were well aware that arguments about socialism and the destruction of capitalism had no appeal whatever to the great mass of the electorate. A politician could win applause, and also votes, inside the Labour party by deploying the rhetoric of socialism; outside the party, among the people at large, this same rhetoric invariably induced hostility or simply boredom. It is worth remarking, though it was little remarked upon at the time, that the campaign against the Common Market in the Labour party and the campaign against it in the country were entirely different campaigns—the one addressed to the majority of the British people, the other to the dwindling band of Labour party faithful.[52]

---

[52] For figures on the extent to which the band of Labour faithful has dwindled, see Dick Leonard, *Paying for Party Politics: The Case for State Subsidies*, PEP Broadsheet, No. 555 (London: Political and Economic Planning, 1975), pp. 2-3. Leonard estimates that the number of individual members of the Labour party fell from just over 1,000,000 in 1953 to between 250,000 and 300,000 in 1973— a fall of between two-thirds and three-quarters. It should be added that the

The anti-Europeans were further constrained by the fact that there was no agreement among them about what, if anything, should replace the Common Market if Britain withdrew from it. Some of them, especially on the left wing of the Labour party, were increasingly of the view that Britain should go it alone: that tariffs, quotas and other restrictions on imports should be used to protect British industry. But others, like Enoch Powell and, some of the time, Peter Shore, held the opposite view: that Britain should seek to negotiate free-trade agreements with the whole of Europe and, ideally, with the United States as well. Given that these views were incompatible, and that none of the alternatives had been thought out in detail, the anti-Marketeers had no real option but to adopt the maxim that attack is the best defense. Theirs, almost inevitably, was a guerrilla campaign, a campaign of harassment. Insofar as it had a common purpose, it was to alarm the electorate about the long-term consequences of Britain's remaining an EEC member.

The most important single consequence to which they drew attention was, of course, the loss of sovereignty inherent in Common Market membership. And, although the opinion polls went on indicating that this was not an issue of much concern to the majority of voters, some anti-Marketeers, notably Enoch Powell and Peter Shore, felt so strongly about it that they made it the main theme of their personal campaigns. Echoes of Hugh Gaitskell's "thousand years of history" could still be heard, particularly in Peter Shore's speeches:

> What the advocates of membership are saying, insistently and insidiously, is that we are finished as a country; that the long and famous story of the British nation and people has ended; that we are now so weak and powerless that we must accept terms and conditions, penalties and limitations, almost as though we had suffered defeat in war; that . . . we have no option but to remain in the Common Market cage.[53]

But most of the anti-Marketeers concentrated on the bread-and-butter aspects of Britain's membership: on rising prices, especially rising food prices; on the threat that the Common Market allegedly posed to British regional policy; on the threat to Scotland and Wales if an

---

memberships of most Western political parties fell over the same period. Leonard reckons that the British Conservative party's membership fell by about a half. What this meant in practice was that a politician who appealed to the party faithful was appealing to a much smaller number of persons than before— and probably to a more unrepresentative number.

[53] *The Times*, May 28, 1975.

ever-increasing share of Britain's economic activity were sucked down into the southeast corner of England, the corner nearest the great continental markets; and—increasingly as the campaign wore on—on the threat to full employment in Britain.

If the dominant figures on the pro-European side were Jenkins and Heath, the dominant figures on the anti-European side were undoubtedly Benn and Powell. They were both likely to provoke controversy; they both therefore attracted the attention of the mass media; they were identified as "personalities." The two men figured prominently in the press coverage of the campaign; they appeared more often on television than anyone else on the anti side.[54] Predictably, it was Tony Benn who provoked one of the few genuinely dramatic incidents of the campaign. Full employment was the issue he chose.

On May 16, just three weeks before polling day, Benn made a speech that he must have known would provoke retaliation from other members of the Labour cabinet.

> Mass unemployment and increasing emigration of our workers and their families to the Continent in search of jobs [Benn said] will be the painful consequence for this country of our continued membership of the European Economic Community. . . . Mr. Heath, who has come back from retirement to lead the European campaign, has given no hint that he understands the horrifying possibility that for the British people EEC membership will mean inhabiting a group of European offshore islands whose industry is permanently unable to provide the jobs and national income to support them.[55]

The reference was to Heath, but the real object of Benn's attack could only be his own colleagues. Two days later, on May 18, he went further, maintaining at a press conference that Britain's EEC membership had already cost the country nearly half a million jobs—

---

[54] Details of the television and press coverage of the campaign are provided by Anthony Smith and Colin Seymour-Ure in chapters 8 and 9 of Butler and Kitzinger, *The 1975 Referendum*. Smith records (p. 194) that the number of appearances by individuals in television broadcasts (feature programs and principal news items) was: Benn, 52; Jenkins, 27; Wilson, 25; Powell, 23; Heath, 23; and Shore, 22. Seymour-Ure documents the extent to which the great majority of newspapers were pro-European both in their editorials and in their news coverage. It is doubtful, however, whether the bias of the press was an important factor in the eventual outcome. After all, the press had been almost as pro-European six years before when the great majority of the electorate had been anti-EEC.

[55] Goodhart, *Full-Hearted Consent*, pp. 159-60.

137,000 directly and a further 360,000 as the result of the deflation needed to offset Britain's trading deficit with the other EEC countries.

If Benn had set out to be provocative, he certainly succeeded. Roy Jenkins suggested derisively that Benn's approach was to think of a figure and then double it. "I find it increasingly difficult," Jenkins said, "to take Mr. Benn seriously as an economics minister." Denis Healey, the chancellor of the exchequer, in one of his few interventions in the campaign, remarked acidly, "When war breaks out, truth is the first casualty." Robert Mellish, Labour's chief whip, described Benn's allegations as "a classic mixture of doubtful logic and raging fantasy." Even the prime minister felt compelled to intervene, reminding both sides that after June 5 "normal collective responsibility and courtesy and comradeship" would be restored, but at the same time dismissing Benn's 500,000-jobs charge. "After going into this as fully as I can," he said, "I believe that the opposite is the truth."[56]

By this time the prime minister had abrogated his rule against pro and anti ministers' appearing together on television, and on June 2, three days before polling day, Benn and Jenkins debated the Common Market issue on the BBC's current affairs program "Panorama." The situation was fraught with danger, but both men seemed to realize that the controversy among ministers had got out of hand and, in front of the cameras, they behaved perfectly civilly towards each other. Indeed in general, despite the Benn episode, the cabinet's agreement to differ proved a considerable success. No one resigned from the cabinet; ministers on the whole confined their public disagreements to the European issue; and, once the referendum was over, normal collective responsibility was, as Wilson hoped it would be, restored almost immediately. The agreement to differ could not, and did not, prevent damage to the Labour party and the Government; but it does seem to have minimized it.[57]

---

[56] The various responses to Benn's speeches are quoted by Goodhart in *Full-Hearted Consent*, pp. 159-61, and by Butler and Kitzinger in *The 1975 Referendum*, pp. 168, 180-82.

[57] The amazing, once contemplated for any length of time, ceases to be amazing, and it is remarkable how quickly the British public, and even British politicians, got used to the spectacle of members of the same Government disagreeing with one another, and even denouncing one another, in public. A rough American equivalent would be if President Carter and Secretary of the Treasury Blumenthal were to suggest in public that Secretary of Commerce Kreps was not wholly honest and Secretary Kreps were to denounce the President and the administration as a whole for pursuing policies that had already increased unemployment and were bound to increase it further. Even in the United States, where politics is considerably more open than in Britain, such events would be regarded as

For the most part, the referendum campaign followed the same course as any ordinary British election campaign. Meetings were held all over the country (many of them well attended); each side had a chance to put its case on television; canvassers distributed leaflets and knocked on doors. The one innovation was the free distribution to every household in the country of three pamphlets: one setting out the "yes" case, one setting out the "no" case, and one setting out the Government's case (which of course was simply another version of the "yes" case). Britain in Europe's pamphlet was largely free of statistics and instead relied on quotations from important British politicians and Commonwealth prime ministers; its theme was that the Community was not perfect but that the safety and prosperity of the country demanded that Britain stay in. The National Referendum Campaign's pamphlet contended that none of the pro-Marketeers' prophesies of higher economic growth if Britain joined the Common Market had been fulfilled; that the Common Market was depriving the British people of their right to self-government; that the Common Market put jobs at risk and led to higher food prices; and that the European Community was far less important to Britain than organizations like NATO, the United Nations, and the Organization for Economic Cooperation and Development. The NRC's pamphlet reminded readers that Norway had voted "no" without suffering any of the dire consequences that the pro-Europeans were predicting if Britain pulled out. The Government's pamphlet, entitled *Britain's New Deal in Europe*, mainly reiterated Britain in Europe's arguments but dwelt at rather greater length on the Labour Government's success in renegotiating the terms. The three pamphlets cost in the order of £1 million to print and distribute and constituted a major additional subsidy to the pro and anti campaigns. According to an opinion poll, fully three-quarters of the electorate saw one or other of the pamphlets. A quarter of the electorate claimed to have read at least one of them from cover to cover.[58]

---

at least worthy of comment. It is not entirely clear why the prime minister abrogated his rule against pro and anti ministers' appearing together on television. It was probably because the rule was having a manifestly distorting effect on the television coverage of the campaign. In any case, by the time the rule was abrogated it no longer seemed important: it was evident that the pro-Europeans were going to win.

[58] For the opinion-poll findings, see Butler and Kitzinger, *The 1975 Referendum*, p. 290. The three pamphlets are reproduced in their entirety by Butler and Kitzinger, pp. 290-304. Since the various British political parties are associated with different colors (the Conservatives mainly with blue, Labour with red, and so on), there was considerable discussion about the colors in which the pamphlets should be printed. In the end, the "yes" pamphlet appeared in a

Benn's démarche on unemployment, or something very like it, had been expected; so had almost all of the other moves made by the two sides. The one genuinely unexpected occurrence of the campaign came during its last week. Edward du Cann, the member of Parliament for Taunton in Somerset, was the chairman of the Conservative backbenchers' "1922 Committee"; he was also a former chairman of the Conservative party and a former minister. Despite an extraordinarily smooth manner, he had the reputation of being a tough politician, much given to calculation. Over the last weekend before polling day, word leaked out that he was about to make a speech claiming that, contrary to what the Conservative party's leaders were saying, at least half of the Conservatives in the country were opposed to Britain's remaining in the EEC. The speech, when it came, amounted to an open appeal to the Conservative rank and file to desert its leaders over Europe. "There is always," du Cann concluded, "a higher loyalty than party loyalty—loyalty to one's country, and what one honestly believes to be her best interests." For a brief moment, it seemed conceivable that du Cann's intervention might have some effect on the outcome; but he was quickly repudiated by the Conservatives' leaders and anyway, whatever his standing in his own party, du Cann was not someone who carried weight in the country. If half the Conservative party's members in the country really were planning to vote "no," evidence of the fact should have emerged months before. None had.[59]

The Campaign's Impact. Between the Dublin summit of March 10-11, 1975, and the eve of poll on June 4, some eleven weeks elapsed. Within a few days of the Dublin summit, the opinion polls were already reporting a lead for the pro-Europeans of roughly two-to-one. On the eve of the poll, the opinion polls were still reporting a lead for the pro-Europeans of roughly two-to-one. The intervening eleven weeks of campaigning appear to have had no significant effect on the intentions of voters, or even on their attitudes towards specific elements in the Common Market controversy. As Table 6-4 shows, between the beginning of April and the beginning of June the "yes" lead fluctuated within fairly wide limits, but at no time did it fall below thirty percentage points. The opinion polls reported that the

---

neutral brown-on-yellow and the "no" pamphlet in an equally neutral yellow-on-brown. The Government's own pamphlet appeared in a patriotic red, white, and blue.

[59] For a full account of the du Cann episode, see Goodhart, *Full-Hearted Consent*, pp. 170-72. It is still not entirely clear what du Cann was up to. For some informed speculation, see Butler and Kitzinger, *The 1975 Referendum*, p. 174.

Table 6-4
REFERENDUM VOTING INTENTIONS, MARCH-JUNE 1975
(in percentages)

Polling Organization	Interviewing Completed	Yes	No	Yes Lead (in percentage points)	(Don't Know) [a]
Forecasts					
ORC	March 2	59	41	18	(18)
Harris	March 9	58	42	16	(22)
ORC	March 9	62	38	24	(26)
Harris	April 6	67	33	34	(18)
ORC	April 6	68	32	36	(12)
Gallup	April 7	65	35	30	(12)
ORC	April 20	67	33	34	(16)
Gallup	April 21	67	33	34	(15)
NOP	April 27	66	34	32	(17)
ORC	April 27	69	31	38	(17)
Harris	May 11	73	27	46	(12)
Gallup	May 12	67	33	34	(11)
Gallup	May 19	68	32	36	(10)
Marplan	May 22	70	30	40	(19)
Gallup	May 27	66	34	32	(10)
Marplan	May 28	72	28	44	(15)
ORC	June 1	72	28	44	(11)
Harris	June 2	73	27	46	(17)
Gallup	June 2	69	31	38	(10)
Marplan	June 3	68	32	36	(15)
Actual Result		67.6	32.4	35.2	

Note: Both the forecasts and the actual referendum result are for Great Britain only; Northern Ireland is not included.

[a] Excluded from the calculation of "yes" and "no" percentages.

Source: The newspapers in which the various polling organizations publish their forecasts are as follows: Opinion Research Centre (ORC), the *Evening Standard;* Louis Harris International, the *Daily Express;* Gallup, the *Daily Telegraph* and the *Sunday Telegraph;* National Opinion Polls (NOP), the *Daily Mail;* and Marplan, *The Sun.*

pro-Europeans were ahead—albeit by differing amounts—in both sexes, in all political parties, in every social class, in every age group, and in every part of the country. The opinion polls also reported that more intending "yes" voters than "no" voters were interested in the outcome of the referendum and that more intending "yes" than "no" voters would "definitely" or "probably" turn out to vote when the time came.[60]

Further evidence for the campaign's limited impact is provided by Table 6-5, which summarizes the results of some of the so-called "quickie" surveys carried out by Louis Harris International for Britain in Europe between mid-May and early June. The Harris organization asked questions repeatedly about all of the major issues raised in the campaign, yet, as Table 6-5 shows, in almost every case the results in early June were almost exactly the same as the results in the middle of May, with only slight variations in between.[61] Tony Benn's statements on unemployment had no discernible effect on the electorate; neither did Edward du Cann's on the state of feeling in the Tory party. Almost the only effect of the campaign seems to have been to change voters' perceptions of whether or not most people in three white Commonwealth countries wanted Britain to remain in Europe. As Table 6-5 shows, the number believing that the balance of opinion in Australia, Canada, and New Zealand was in favor of Britain's staying in rose quite strikingly, from 30 percent on May 15 to 41 percent on June 3. Britain in Europe spent almost £1.5 million on the campaign. It is ironic to reflect that the only material result of all this expenditure may have been marginally to increase the British public's knowledge of the state of public opinion in three foreign countries— none of them in Europe and none of them less than 3,000 miles away.

On the evening of Wednesday, June 4, with the polls due to open in only a few hours' time, there could be no real doubt about the outcome of the referendum. The pro-Europeans had won. But there could still be detected a certain nervousness on the pro-European side. Quite apart from the nervousness that all politicians feel on the eve of every election, many pro-Europeans were worried that either a very low turnout or an unexpectedly low margin of victory might deprive them of the overwhelming moral victory that they sought— and, worse, encourage the anti-Europeans to find some means of fighting on. The pro-Europeans wanted terribly to win, and to be

---

[60] For example, the Gallup Poll found in mid-May that 84 percent of intending "yes" voters were "very or moderately interested" in the campaign, compared with only 71 percent of intending "no" voters. Similarly, 88 percent of "yes" voters said that they would "definitely" or "probably" turn out to vote, compared with 78 percent of "no" voters. See the *Sunday Telegraph*, May 18, 1975.

[61] It should be borne in mind, reading Table 6-5, that the samples interviewed in these "quickie" surveys were small (about 650) and that the results are therefore very liable to sampling error. But there is no reason to suppose that the general picture produced by these surveys is seriously distorted.

125

Table 6-5

BELIEFS ABOUT THE CONSEQUENCES OF BRITAIN'S STAYING IN OR LEAVING THE COMMON MARKET
(in percentages)

Q: Do you think *unemployment* in Britain will go up faster if we stay in the Common Market or if we leave it?

	May 13	May 23	May 27	June 3
Faster if we stay in	23	19	23	22
Faster if we leave	25	22	31	23
Same/no difference	38	40	36	39
Don't know	14	19	10	16

Q: Do you think the British Government will have *more influence* on important things affecting Britain if we stay in the Common Market or if we leave it?

	May 13	May 24	May 28	June 2
More influence if we stay in	38	34	30	37
More influence if we leave	31	32	31	28
Same/no difference	17	23	26	20
Don't know	14	11	13	15

Q: In the long run, do you think we will be *better off* if we stay in the Common Market or if we leave it?

	May 13	May 24	May 29	May 31
Better off if we stay	60	57	55	59
Better off if we leave	27	28	27	24
Same/no difference	2	5	7	5
Don't know	11	10	11	12

Q: Do you think *food prices* in Britain will go up faster if we stay in the Common Market or if we leave it?

	May 13	May 24	May 27	May 31
Faster if we stay in	39	38	36	38
Faster if we leave	16	14	15	13
Same/no difference	33	35	41	37
Don't know	12	12	8	11

Q: Do you think it will be easier to deal with Britain's *economic problems* if we stay in the Common Market or if we leave it?

	May 13	May 23	May 27	June 2
Easier if we stay in	47	42	48	45
Easier if we leave	30	22	25	25
Same/no difference	9	19	17	17
Don't know	14	17	10	13

Q: Do you think most people in Australia, Canada and New Zealand want us to leave the Common Market or stay in it?

	May 15	May 23	May 27	June 3
Want us to leave	33	32	29	25
Want us to stay in	30	37	32	41
Don't know	37	31	39	34

Q: Who do you have more confidence in: the political leaders who want Britain to stay in the Common Market, or the political leaders who want Britain to leave it?

	May 20	May 27	June 2
Pro-Market politicians	45	42	45
Anti-Market politicians	22	23	21
Neither/both equally	23	28	26
Don't know	10	7	8

Source: Louis Harris International, "Fourteenth 'Quickie' of the Referendum Campaign for Britain in Europe: Results of Tuesday's Survey, June 3rd," 47515/14, pp. 2-3.

seen to have won. As Roy Jenkins put it at the final Britain in Europe press conference, referring to his opponents:

What they hope for is a low turnout and a relatively narrow margin on the basis of which they can continue the struggle, prolong the uncertainty and try to prevent Britain from playing an effective, constructive and influential role within the Community. Let us vote decisively to settle the issue overwhelmingly and to free us from the continued debilitation of being hesitant and reluctant partners.[62]

When the polls closed at 10 o'clock on the evening of June 5, the real question was not who had won but whether Roy Jenkins's wish had been fulfilled.

[62] *The Times,* June 5, 1975.

7
THE DENOUEMENT

The outcome of the Common Market referendum was largely determined by the success of Britain's renegotiations with the other eight members of the Community, which enabled a Labour Government to join with the Conservative and Liberal parties in recommending a "yes" vote to the British electorate. Once it was clear that such a recommendation would be forthcoming, the majority of voters let it be known, via the opinion polls, that they were now in favor of Britain's continued membership in the EEC—or at least that they were reconciled to it. The turning point was the Dublin summit; the referendum campaign itself made little or no difference. As we saw in the last chapter, if the referendum had been held in early April instead of in early June, the result would almost certainly have been the same. It does not, however, follow that the result of the referendum was of no significance. An earthquake does not cease to be an earthquake simply because it has been widely anticipated. On the contrary, as we shall see later in this chapter, the referendum on the Common Market was one of the half-dozen most important events in postwar British history—in terms of what it made possible and, even more important, in terms of what it prevented.[1]

Polling day was Thursday, June 5, and in an ordinary British election most of the votes would have been counted that night and the results declared straightaway. But because the votes were being counted not constituency by constituency but on a county and re-

[1] The reader is entitled to ask what the other five "most important" events were. In the author's judgment, they were the election of the Labour Government in 1945, the granting of independence to India in 1947, the failure of the Suez expedition of 1956, the post-1959 Conservative Government's decolonization of Africa, and the defeat of the Heath Government by the miners (and the electorate) in 1974.

gional basis, the night of June 5–6 was given over to collecting the ballot papers at district centers and to checking their validity. The business of making a tally of the "yeses" and the "noes" did not begin until nine o'clock the next morning. The first result, from the Scilly Isles, with a population of only a few hundred, was declared at 11:00 A.M. on Friday; the results from two rural counties, one in northern England and one in Wales, came in soon afterwards. From the beginning it was clear that Roy Jenkins's wish had indeed been fulfilled. Turnout was reasonably high, 64.5 percent, and the result was an overwhelming pro-European victory, 67.2 percent to 32.8 percent—a margin in absolute terms of nearly 9 million votes. Moreover, the victory was a nationwide victory. England voted "yes," Wales voted "yes," Scotland voted "yes," even Northern Ireland voted "yes" (though on a low turnout and by a narrow margin).[2] Of the sixty-eight counting units over the country as a whole, no fewer than sixty-six returned pro-European majorities. Both of the two that did not, Shetland and the Western Isles in Scotland, had tiny electorates.[3] It was calculated later that if the count had been conducted on a constituency-by-constituency basis, as many of the anti-Europeans had originally wanted, only 4 or 5, at most, of the country's 635 parliamentary constituencies would have been seen to have voted "no."[4]

The results are set out fully in the Appendix and have been analyzed at considerable length by Butler and Kitzinger.[5] There is no need to go into detail here. But three points are worth making.

---

[2] Northern Ireland had been widely expected to vote "no." Many of the Republican groups were advocating a "no" vote, and so were some of the militant Protestant groups, led by the Rev. Ian Paisley. Paisley thought that the Common Market was a Popish plot. The result in Ulster was something of a comment on the view taken by the citizens of the province of their more extreme leaders. The turnout, however, was only 47.4 percent, the "yes" vote only 52.1 percent.

[3] Orkney and Shetland, and the Western Isles, are the two most isolated parts of the United Kingdom. The nearest railway station to the Shetland islands is Bergen in Norway. The parliamentary constituency of Orkney and Shetland has an electorate of only about 26,000; the electorate of the Shetland islands alone is only about 13,000. The electorate of the Western Isles is a mere 22,000. Shetland probably voted "no" partly because the Shetland islanders feel themselves to be a distinct community, more closely related to the Norse seafarers of old than to the modern Scots. They may also have been worried about the future of the fishing industry. The people of the Western Isles may well have been influenced by the views of their Scottish Nationalist M.P., Donald Stewart.

[4] See Martin Collins, "Who Voted What" in Roger Jowell and Gerald Hoinville, eds., *Britain into Europe: Public Opinion and the EEC 1961-75* (London: Croom Helm, 1976), pp. 106-8.

[5] Butler and Kitzinger, *The 1975 Referendum*, pp. 263-73.

The first is that it is hard to know what significance to read into the turnout figure of 64.5 percent.[6] On the one hand, the turnout figure was rather low in comparison with that in the other countries that also held Common Market referenda; in Norway the turnout was 79.2 percent, in Denmark 90.1 percent, in Ireland 71.0 percent.[7] On the other hand, the turnout was much higher than many people had expected, given voters' lack of interest in the Common Market and the predictability of the outcome. Should one seek to explain why the turnout was so high, or why it was not even higher? In the absence of a general theory about voting turnout in British referenda, it is impossible to be sure.

The second point concerns the quite remarkable uniformity of the results over the country as a whole. Not only did almost every part of the United Kingdom vote "yes"; the margin of the pro-Europeans' victory varied within quite narrow limits. Apart from Shetland, the Western Isles, and Northern Ireland, no county or region recorded a "yes" vote of less than 54.6 percent or more than 76.3 percent; the vast majority of counties and regions, more than two-thirds, fell into the 65–75 percent range. Wales (66.5 percent "yes") was scarcely less pro-European than England (68.7 percent), and even Scotland (58.4 percent) produced a "yes" result that only a year before would have seemed beyond the pro-Europeans' wildest dreams. As Butler and Kitzinger remark, "It was a national argument, a national campaign . . . and a national result."[8]

The third point is related to the second. To the extent that there were variations between different localities and different regions of the country, the explanation lies hardly at all in local circumstances and almost entirely in nationwide differences of partisanship and class. The opinion polls reported that more Conservative voters than Labour voters were pro-European. Predictably, therefore, Conservative parts of the country produced larger "yes" majorities than Labour parts of the country. Every one of the dozen English counties that recorded the largest Conservative votes at the October 1974 general election now returned "yes" majorities above the English average; the "yes" vote in heavily Conservative North Yorkshire was the

---

[6] The National Counting Office decided to make an estimate of how many of those on the electoral register had in fact died and, on the basis of this estimate, returned a somewhat higher turnout figure of 65.0 percent. The turnout at the previous general election was 72.8 percent. See Butler and Kitzinger, *The 1975 Referendum*, p. 263, n. 2.

[7] Stanley Alderson, *Yea or Nay?: Referenda in the United Kingdom* (London: Cassell, 1975), pp. 53–54.

[8] Butler and Kitzinger, *The 1975 Referendum*, p. 272.

largest in the country, 76.3 percent. By contrast, of the dozen English counties that recorded the largest Labour votes in October 1974, all but one now produced "yes" majorities that were below average. Similarly, just as Conservative counties were more pro-European than Labour counties, so middle-class counties (many of them the same ones) were more pro-European than working-class counties. Of the dozen counties with the largest proportions of nonmanual workers in England, nine recorded above-average "yes" votes. By contrast, eight of the twelve counties with the lowest proportions of non-manual workers recorded below-average "yes" votes (three of the four exceptions being largely rural counties, with only relatively small urban working-class populations).[9]

Opinion surveys conducted just before polling day provide additional evidence of the levels of support for continued British EEC membership in different sections of the population. Table 7-1 reports the results of one such survey.[10] It reinforces the point that "no" strength was at its greatest among Labour voters and manual workers; but it also shows that, despite the best efforts of the Labour party outside Parliament and of prominent trade union leaders like Jack Jones and Hugh Scanlon, the majority of Labour voters, manual workers, and trade union members were still to be found in the "yes" camp. The pro-Europeans' victory was nationwide, not merely geographically but also socially.

---

[9] The calculations in this paragraph have been made from data supplied by Butler and Kitzinger in *The 1975 Referendum*, pp. 266-69. The dozen most Conservative counties, with their "yes" percentages, were: North Yorkshire (76.3), Surrey (76.2), West Sussex (76.2), Buckinghamshire (74.3), East Sussex (74.3), Oxfordshire (73.6), Dorset (73.5), Hereford and Worcester (72.8), Suffolk (72.2), Devon (72.1), Gloucestershire (71.7), and Hampshire (71.0). The dozen most Labour counties, with their "yes" percentages, were: Tyne and Wear (62.9), South Yorkshire (63.4), Durham (64.2), Greater Manchester (64.5), Merseyside (64.8), West Midlands (65.1), West Yorkshire (65.4), Nottinghamshire (66.8), Cleveland (67.3), Staffordshire (67.4), Derbyshire (68.6), and Northumberland (69.2). Only Northumberland was above the English average of 68.7. The dozen most nonmanual counties, with their "yes" percentages, were: West Sussex (76.2), East Sussex (74.3), Buckinghamshire (74.3), Oxford-shire (73.6), Dorset (73.5), Berkshire (72.6), Kent (70.4), Hertfordshire (70.4), Isle of Wight (70.2), Avon (67.8), Essex (67.6) and Greater London (66.7). The dozen most manual counties, with their "yes" percentages, were: South York-shire (63.4), Durham (64.2), West Midlands (65.1), West Yorkshire (65.4), Nottinghamshire (66.8), Cleveland (67.3), Staffordshire (67.4), Derbyshire (68.6), Northumberland (69.2), Northamptonshire (69.5), the Scilly Isles (74.5), and Lincolnshire (74.7). The three rural counties referred to in the text are North-umberland, the Scilly Isles, and Lincolnshire.

[10] Table 7-1 can be compared with the table, based on Gallup Poll data, given in Butler and Kitzinger, *The 1975 Referendum*, p. 252. The findings reported in the two tables are very similar.

Table 7-1

REFERENDUM VOTING INTENTIONS BY SEX, AGE, PARTY,
CLASS, AND UNION MEMBERSHIP
(in percentages)

	Yes	No	Undecided, etc.
All Voters [a]	64	25	11
Sex			
Male	63	28	9
Female	65	22	13
Age			
18-24	59	27	14
25-44	65	24	11
45-64	65	25	10
65+	61	23	16
Party			
Conservative	82	12	6
Labour	52	35	13
Liberal	64	29	7
Class			
AB	85	8	7
C1	70	21	9
C2	56	32	12
DE	55	29	16
Union Members	56	34	10

Note: The interviews were carried out on May 27 and 28, 1975.
[a] Not including Northern Ireland.
[b] See Table 2-2, footnote a.
Source: Louis Harris International, "Second 'State of the Battle' Survey," May 30, 1975, 47517, p. 5.

Tony Benn responded to the result by holding an impromptu press conference in the front garden of his London home. His American wife was at his side. Benn's moral position was almost as weak as it seemed, but not quite. He had campaigned against the Common Market, but equally he had been largely responsible for the fact that the referendum had been held at all—for the fact that the people had been consulted. At his press conference populist Benn, predictably, took precedence over anti-Marketeer Benn:

I have just been in receipt of a very big message from the British people. I read it loud and clear. It is clear that by an overwhelming majority the British people have voted to stay in, and I am sure everybody would want to accept that. That has been the principle of all of us who have advocated the referendum.[11]

Peter Shore likewise indicated that, while he was disappointed by the result, he accepted that it was binding on the Government and therefore on himself.[12]

Only Enoch Powell among the prominent anti-Marketeers refused to accept the people's verdict. He refused to believe that the British people would, or could, be absorbed into a federal Europe:

> If I were young, I should despair, but I do not. I am convinced that in this referendum the vast majority of those voting had no notion that they were saying Yes or No to Britain continuing as a nation at all. The fault did not lie with many of the advocates of British membership who declared candidly that the nation state was obsolete and that Britain therefore must become a province in a new European state and cease to be a self-governing nation.
>
> So incredible was this, however, to most people that the words simply bounced off them; they had no meaning in their ears. Now what will happen is that gradually, and perhaps not so gradually, it will come home to them that their Yes vote to Europe was No to Britain as a nation.[13]

Powell thought the people's verdict was reversible, and would be reversed.

The pro-Europeans were delighted with the result. Although a 67.2 percent "yes" vote on a 64.5 percent turnout meant that rather less than half of the total eligible electorate had voted for Europe, the result was completely convincing and came as a great relief after the more than five years during which the opinion polls had continuously reported substantial anti-European majorities. The headlines in the popular newspapers captured the pro-Europeans' mood: "YES! MILLION TIMES YES" (*Evening Standard*), "MESSAGE RECEIVED" (*Daily Mirror*), "EUROPEANS!" (*Daily Express*), "YES!" (*Daily Mail*), and "GOOD! NOW LET'S ALL GET CRACKING" (*The Sun*). Roy Jenkins, speaking in the course of Britain in Europe's day-long celebration party at the Waldorf Hotel, recalled that June 6, 1975, was the thirty-first anniversary of D-Day. He described the result as "a second D-Day for British resurgence in Europe based not on sulky

---

[11] *The Times*, June 7, 1975.
[12] *Guardian*, June 7, 1975.
[13] *Daily Mail*, June 7, 1975.

acquiescence but on enthusiastic cooperation."[14] Edward Heath said that referendum day had been a great day for him, a great day for Britain, and a great day for Europe. "The referendum has completely endorsed everything we've done," he said of his own Government, "and everything I did as Prime Minister."[15] Every daily newspaper except the Communist *Morning Star* welcomed the result, most of them making the point that it was a necessary, though not a sufficient, condition of Britain's economic recovery. Rather surprisingly, it was left to the strongly Conservative *Daily Telegraph* to acknowledge that the pro-Europeans' victory was also Harold Wilson's:

> The result of the referendum is, quite frankly, a triumph for Mr. Wilson. In deciding to take up Mr. Benn's challenge, he must surely have known that he was taking a great political gamble—given that, first, he wanted Britain to stay in the Market, and second, that a referendum was the only hope of achieving that result without the Labour party disintegrating. His gamble has paid off handsomely, perhaps even better than he had ever dared hope in the watches of the night. Because it has come out right, Mr. Wilson deserves the credit.[16]

At least as important as the reactions in Britain were the reactions on the Continent. The governments of the other eight members of the Community remained officially silent, taking the view that it was not for them to pronounce on a matter of domestic British politics. But Helmut Schmidt, the West German chancellor, spoke of the German people's "satisfaction and joy," and Jean Sauvagnargues, the French foreign minister, similarly made public his "satisfaction at the positive result."[17] But most politicians on the Continent, like many in Britain, were probably more relieved at the outcome than positively enthusiastic. The British had over the years become faintly tiresome in the eyes of the continentals, what with their comings and goings and their insistence on renegotiating what had already been negotiated. As *The Times*'s correspondent in Brussels put it:

> The decision was warmly and unsurprisingly applauded by the European Commission. But the popping of champagne corks could not disguise a certain weariness and irritation

---

[14] *The Times*, June 7, 1975.
[15] *Guardian*, June 7, 1975.
[16] *Daily Telegraph*, June 7, 1975.
[17] Ibid.

with the whole referendum exercise, which, despite moments of nervousness, was never taken very seriously in Brussels.

The motives behind the referendum were seen as relating solely to the internal politics of the British Labour party, and no one in recent months . . . considered that there was any real danger of a "no" vote.

Nevertheless, as *The Times*'s correspondent added, "the size of the majority brought genuine pleasure and relief."[18]

There is a certain temptation to agree with the world-weary commissioners of Brussels and to conclude that the 1975 Common Market referendum did not really matter all that much—that it was little more than a formality, something that had to be gone through, perhaps, but not something of great intrinsic significance. Butler and Kitzinger, in their authoritative study of the referendum, seem inclined towards this point of view:

The verdict of the referendum must be kept in perspective.

Nor should the psychological impact of the referendum result in Britain be over-estimated.

As far as the ongoing processes of British party politics were concerned, the effects of the referendum seemed by the end of 1975 to be much smaller than most observers had expected.[19]

And, up to a point, Butler and Kitzinger are clearly right. The referendum did not reveal profound depths of pro-European enthusiasm in the British people. It did not lead to the formation of a coalition Government. It did not upset the balance of power in the Labour party. It did not cause Britain suddenly to become a sort of 1930s-style plebiscitary democracy. For better or worse, British politics—and indeed European politics generally—flowed on after June 5, 1975, much as they had done before.

Yet it would be quite wrong to underestimate the referendum's significance. In the first place, one has to distinguish between the consequences of the fact that the referendum was held at all and the consequences of its having turned out the way it did. In the second place, one has to distinguish between the consequences of the referendum's having turned out as it did and the consequences that would have followed if it had turned out in some other way. The non-

---

[18] *The Times*, June 7, 1975.

[19] Butler and Kitzinger, *The 1975 Referendum*, pp. 280-81.

events of history are, after all, sometimes more important than the events that actually occur.

The chief consequence of the referendum's having been held at all was that it made the holding of future referenda in Britain much more likely. The referendum had worked; it had gone smoothly. The genie had been let out of the bottle, and nothing very terrible had happened. A new option was therefore open to any Government that was as deeply divided as the Labour Government had been in 1975, or that wanted for any reason to elicit an authoritative statement of the people's views. The obvious immediate candidate for a further referendum—or series of referenda—was the political future of Scotland and Wales. Did the people of Scotland and Wales want substantial powers to be devolved from the central government in Westminster onto subordinate national assemblies? Or, alternatively, did they want complete independence? To put it another way, how far were the Scottish and Welsh nationalist parties, in demanding independence, genuinely speaking for the peoples that they claimed to represent? The only possible way of obtaining authoritative answers to these questions, it could be argued, was by means of referenda. It is a striking fact that, within weeks of the Common Market referendum, a number of senior politicians, including Edward Heath, were maintaining that referenda should be held in Scotland and Wales; and in the event the Labour Government announced in the House of Commons on December 13, 1976, that there would be referenda sometime during the following year.[20] It is possible, of course, that referenda in Scotland and Wales would have been held even without the Common Market precedent, but it seems unlikely.

The most important single consequence of Britain's "yes" vote on June 5, 1975, was to place Britain's membership in the Common Market beyond any doubt. The fact that the vote was a democratic one, together with the size of the pro-European majority, gave Britain's membership in the EEC a legitimacy that nothing else could possibly have done. The question of British Common Market membership had been on Britain's political agenda for nearly a generation. Suddenly, and permanently, it was struck off. The parliamentary Labour party, which had hitherto boycotted the European Parliament in Strasbourg, now decided to send a delegation. The Trades Union Congress, which had hitherto boycotted the institutions of the EEC, now decided to participate in them. The anti-European ministers in the Government, many of whom had taken advantage of their

---

[20] *The Times*, December 14, 1976.

positions to obstruct EEC initiatives, now felt obliged to cooperate. Indeed for the anti-Europeans as a whole the referendum had badly boomeranged. A cartoon in the *Observer* depicted Tony Benn as a cowboy trying to lasso Harold Wilson. The lasso, as it flew through the air, spelled out the word "Referendum." But the neck that the lasso's noose was about to encircle was Tony Benn's. Another cartoon in the same newspaper, published on the Sunday following the referendum, showed Tony Benn as a very large cat about to swallow Harold Wilson, depicted as a diminutive, pipe-smoking canary. But in the end it was the canary, much enlarged in size, that had swallowed the cat.[21]

All of the anti-Europeans suffered a severe loss of political credibility. Enoch Powell faded even further into the political background.[22] The Scottish and Welsh nationalists were seen to have been rebuffed by the Scottish and Welsh peoples. The hollowness of the Labour left's claim to speak on behalf of "the people" as a whole was exposed in the most ruthless possible manner. But the chief sufferer, as the *Observer*'s cartoons implied, was Tony Benn. Before the referendum, he had been widely regarded as the coming man of British politics. He was an inspiration to many on the left wing of the Labour party; he was a sort of bogeyman to many others, both inside the party and out. After the referendum, he virtually disappeared from view. He meekly accepted demotion from the Department of Industry to the Department of Energy. When the

---

[21] *Observer*, June 1 and 8, 1975.

[22] Powell had effectively deprived himself of a political base by refusing to stand as a Conservative candidate in February 1974, though he subsequently returned to Parliament as the United Ulster Unionist member for South Down. His speeches on immigration and race relations, his refusal to stand in February 1974, and his broad hint to voters that they should vote Labour rather than see the Conservatives hand over British sovereignty to the Common Market together alienated the bulk of the Conservative party. He was in any case anathema to the great majority of the Labour party. His acceptance of a seat in Northern Ireland removed him from the mainstream of British party politics, and at the same time, since he was bound to have to appeal to Protestant loyalist sentiment in Ulster, meant that he would be expressing sentiments that would find little echo in Great Britain. Powell has created such a stir in Britain and has such a large following that it is often forgotten that he also has a large "anti-following." The Louis Harris poll referred to on p. 112 above found that 33 percent of the electorate liked and respected Powell; but it also found that 31 percent of the electorate disliked and distrusted him. His dislike-and-distrust figure was higher than for any other major figure except Tony Benn (32 percent). His like-and-respect figure, to be sure, was higher than that for any other anti-Marketeer, but it was not as high as that for several of the pro-Marketeers: 33 percent compared with 42 percent for Wilson and Heath, and 40 percent for the then leader of the Liberal party, Jeremy Thorpe.

Labour party held its leadership election during the following year, after the retirement of Harold Wilson, he could secure only 37 out of 314 votes from the parliamentary Labour party and stood down after the first ballot. It will never be known whether the referendum actually diminished Benn's political strength or whether it merely showed that his strength had been exaggerated all along. Either way it brought to an abrupt end, at least for the time being, the brief "Benn era" in British political history.[23]

Nevertheless, Butler and Kitzinger are right to point out that the effects of the referendum on the structure of British party politics were not as great as many observers had predicted—or, in many cases, hoped. In particular, the referendum did not dislodge the radical left from its positions of power in the Labour party, especially in the extraparliamentary Labour party. The left had been publicly humiliated; but that did not mean that it lost its seats on the executives of powerful trade unions, or its seats on the Labour party's National Executive Committee, or its preponderance of votes at Labour party conferences. If the Labour party had been an outward-looking organization, a body concerned with maximizing its appeal to the mass electorate, then the referendum might well have had the effect of causing it to take up more moderate policy positions and to elect a less radical, more moderate Executive—just as the American Democratic party, having made the mistake of nominating a George McGovern in 1972, nominated a Jimmy Carter in 1976. But by the mid-1970s the machinery of the Labour party was largely—though perhaps only temporarily—in the hands of "true believers," of men and women for whom fighting for the ultimate triumph of socialism was far more important than fighting

---

[23] It is easy only two or three years later to forget that during Labour's years in opposition 1970-74 and, even more, during the first year of the new Labour Government Benn was the most talked about, and most feared, figure in British public life. Although he was unpopular with the electorate and even with many Labour M.P.s, his enormous capacity for hard work and his willingness, whatever the issue, to say exactly what the rank and file of the Labour party wanted to hear gave him great power within the party and, through the party, within the Labour Government. Many leading figures in the party, including Wilson, did not think much of him and wanted to put him in his place. The referendum gave them their chance. By contrast, Michael Foot, although he had once been far to the left of Benn, was sobered by the experience of government and in any case was more disposed than Benn to be loyal to the Labour Government. His standing in the parliamentary Labour party and among his cabinet colleagues steadily rose, and he was eventually elected deputy leader of the party in October 1976. His election, however, did not make him the heir apparent to Callaghan; as it happens, no deputy leader of the Labour party has ever become leader.

and winning democratic elections.[24] It was left to the Labour party inside Parliament to concern itself with trying to win elections—and also with trying to govern the country.

If this were all that there were to be said, then one might be entitled to conclude that the referendum had indeed been largely a formality. After all, the arrival of a delegation of British Labour M.P.s at Strasbourg did not suddenly enhance the power and prestige of the European Parliament; the demotion of a single British cabinet minister, however much it may have been desired by large numbers of people, is not exactly the stuff of which history is made.

There is, however, more to be said—a good deal more. To end our story at this point would be rather like saying that the only consequence of the 1962 Cuban missile crisis was the signing of the nuclear test ban treaty, thereby ignoring completely the death and destruction that would almost certainly have followed if the crisis had turned out differently. The question we ought to go on to ask about the Common Market referendum is: What would have happened if it had turned out differently, if the British people's answer on June 5, 1975, had been "no" to Europe instead of "yes"?

Our answers to this question must necessarily be speculative; but one thing is certain. If the British people had voted "no" on June 5, they would have been repudiating, consciously, both the House of Commons, which over a period of fourteen years had consistently voted in favor of EEC membership, and also the leaders of all three of the country's major political parties. They would have been saying "no," not just to Europe but to almost all of those who had been the country's political leaders since after the Second World War. The moral effect of such a repudiation would have been tremendous. It would have called into question the way in which Britain's parliamentary institutions had functioned until then. It would have undermined the moral authority of any Government formed from among the country's existing political leaders. It would have strengthened the political positions of the extreme left and the extreme right. It would have had the most profound effects on Britain's standing overseas. Britain, with all of its economic difficulties,

---

[24] It was a stroke of luck for the left that Labour was returned to power in 1974. As the result of Labour's return to power, it could claim that Labour had a "mandate" from the electorate to enact all of the policies that the party had adopted in opposition between 1970 and 1974. In fact, Labour's 1974 victories owed nothing to the party's policies and everything to the unpopularity of the Conservatives and the vagaries of the electoral system. See Penniman, ed., *Britain at the Polls.*

would suddenly have seemed a very doubtful proposition politically as well.

Moreover, a "no" vote would have placed the Labour Government in an extraordinarily invidious—perhaps impossible—position. Harold Wilson and James Callaghan had said that they would abide by the result of the referendum, and undoubtedly they meant what they said. So did most of the other members of the cabinet. Suppose that they and their senior colleagues had conscientiously set about trying to withdraw Britain from the European Community. The country and the world would have been treated to the extraordinary spectacle of a British Government seeking to carry out a policy that was the exact opposite of the policy that it had until recently claimed to believe in. The Government's own pamphlet during the referendum campaign had told the British people that, in the Government's view, if Britain were to give up membership of the European Community, "the effect could only be damaging."[25] The Government would now be seeking to carry out a policy that, on its own admission, would be damaging to Britain's interests. The spectacle would, at the very least, have been a little undignified.

But it is by no means clear that the Labour Government could have carried out such a policy. Shirley Williams and Roy Jenkins had both said that they would resign from the Government rather than be parties to Britain's withdrawal from the EEC. Undoubtedly they, too, meant what they said. If they had resigned, a number of other ministers—one or two from inside the cabinet, possibly as many as a dozen from outside—would have resigned with them. The resigning ministers would have had considerable support from among the large number of pro-Europeans on the Labour back benches. Under these circumstances, there is a good chance that the Labour Government would have been unable to carry on.

Even if it had been able to carry on, it might have found it impossible to enact the legislation that would have been required to withdraw Britain from the European Community. After all, the House of Commons had, as recently as April 9, 1975, voted by 398 votes to 172 in favor of accepting the renegotiated terms of entry. If the House of Commons was to pass a bill taking Britain out of the Community, more than a hundred members of Parliament who had voted in favor of Europe in the spring would now have to be prepared to vote against it during the following autumn and winter. It was not at all clear that so many members would be ready to

---

[25] See Butler and Kitzinger, *The 1975 Referendum*, p. 289.

switch their votes, even in response to the declared will of the people. They would, moreover, have to be prepared to switch their votes not once but many times. During the first seven months of 1972, while the original European Communities Bill was passing through Parliament, the House of Commons had voted on no fewer than 104 occasions on matters related to Britain's accession to the EEC.[26] The number of votes that would now be required would be at least as great—probably even greater since Britain had by now been a full member of the EEC for more than two years. The chances of the Government's majority being gradually eaten away were considerable. It goes without saying, on top of all this, that, if the "no" vote on June 5 had been carried by a very small majority or on a very low poll, the Government's difficulties in passing its withdrawal legislation through Parliament would have been greater still.

Even if the Labour Government had been able to maintain itself in power and even if it had been able to secure a parliamentary majority for withdrawing Britain from Europe, the amount of governmental time and energy that would have been consumed would have been vast. Many senior cabinet ministers would have spent most of their time doing nothing else. The holding of the referendum had already distracted the Government for several months from dealing with the urgent economic problems confronting the country, especially inflation. If the vote had been "no" on June 5, the Government would have gone on being distracted for a further six months at least, probably for much longer. By the summer of 1975 British decision making and Community decision making had penetrated each other deeply. In the fields of agriculture, transport, energy, immigration, regional policy, and trade, the British policy-making process was increasingly part of the European policy-making process; more and more substantive British policy decisions did not make sense except in European terms. Britain could undoubtedly have withdrawn from the EEC, even in 1975; but it would have been less like the United States withdrawing from the United Nations and more like Illinois, Indiana, and Ohio withdrawing from the United States. The process of withdrawal, in itself, would have been extremely costly.

The effects that a "no" vote would have had on the Labour party are harder to calculate. They might well have been cataclysmic. Popular rejection of the Government's recommendation would seriously have weakened the positions of Wilson and Callaghan, the chief architects of the recommendation. It would, by the same token,

---

[26] Kitzinger, *Diplomacy and Persuasion*, p. 386.

have greatly strengthened the positions of Tony Benn and Michael Foot. One or the other would have become at once the heir apparent to the Labour leadership. Had Benn or Foot subsequently become Labour leader, Labour's electoral prospects would undoubtedly have deteriorated—unless of course their standing with the public had improved substantially since the time of the referendum. At the same time, the party as well as the Government would have been weakened by the resignation of Roy Jenkins, Shirley Williams, and other prominent pro-Marketeers—that is, of many of the Labour party's most widely liked and respected figures. Taken together, the election of Benn or Foot and the departure of Jenkins and Williams could quite conceivably have precipitated a permanent split in the party between the moderate center and the more extreme left, effectively ruling out any chance of Labour's being returned to power for at least a generation.

These political consequences of a "no" vote—and, although all of them are speculative, some at least would have been bound to occur—would have been serious enough. Yet they pale into insignificance compared with the effects that a "no" vote would have had on the economy. This is not the place to consider the probable economic consequences in detail, but it seems fair to say that they would have included: a sharp fall in the value of sterling (almost certainly a much sharper fall than in fact occurred in 1976); an equally sharp fall in Britain's overseas credit worthiness; a decline in investment by British businesses as the result of the loss of confidence that would have been caused by a "no" vote; a decline in foreign investment in Britain as the result of both the loss of confidence and of free British access to EEC markets; a deterioration in the balance-of-payments position; and, as the result of all of these factors, an acceleration of inflation and a rise in unemployment. Britain's economic position was already parlous in 1975. One cannot know for sure, but it seems highly probable that a "no" vote on June 5 would have precipitated something approaching an economic disaster.

Quite apart from the tangible consequences that a "no" vote would have had, it would have revealed something rather frightening about the mood of the British people. It would have revealed that the British people had not come to terms with Britain's decline as a world power over the previous thirty years; that they had not ultimately reconciled themselves to the loss of empire; that in the interdependent world of the 1970s they still fondly imagined that Britain could go it alone; that confronted with a crisis they were a people who would turn in upon themselves rather than face reality. Conversely, the size of the British people's "yes" vote on June 5 indicated that, despite everything, they remained an outward-looking people, a people who had not lost faith either in their leaders or in themselves.

The British Common Market referendum of 1975 did not change the course of history, but it did prevent the course of history from being changed—almost certainly for the worse.

APPENDIX:
Results of the Referendum on the
Common Market, June 5, 1975

(in percentages)

	Turnout	Yes	No	Yes Lead (in percentage points)
United Kingdom	64.5	67.2	32.8	34.4
England	64.6	68.7	31.3	37.4
Wales	66.7	66.5	33.5	33.0
Scotland	61.7	58.4	41.6	16.8
Northern Ireland	47.4	52.1	47.9	4.2
English Counties				
Avon	68.7	67.8	32.2	35.6
Bedfordshire	67.9	69.4	30.6	38.8
Berkshire	66.4	72.6	27.4	45.2
Buckinghamshire	69.5	74.3	25.7	48.6
Cambridgeshire	62.2	74.1	25.9	48.2
Cheshire	65.5	70.1	29.9	40.2
Cleveland	60.2	67.3	32.7	34.6
Cornwall	66.8	68.5	31.5	37.0
Cumbria	64.8	71.9	28.1	43.8
Derbyshire	64.1	68.6	31.4	37.2
Devon	68.0	72.1	27.9	44.2
Dorset	68.3	73.5	26.5	47.0
Durham	61.5	64.2	35.8	28.4
Essex	67.7	67.6	32.4	35.2
Gloucestershire	68.4	71.7	28.3	43.4
Greater London	60.8	66.7	33.3	33.4
Greater Manchester	64.1	64.5	35.5	29.0
Hampshire	68.0	71.0	29.0	42.0
Hereford and Worcester	66.4	72.8	27.2	45.6
Hertfordshire	70.2	70.4	29.6	40.8

	Turnout	Yes	No	Yes Lead (in percentage points)
Humberside	62.4	67.8	32.2	35.6
Isles of Scilly	75.0	74.5	25.5	49.0
Isle of Wight	67.5	70.2	29.8	40.4
Kent	67.4	70.4	29.6	40.8
Lancashire	66.4	68.6	31.4	37.2
Leicestershire	67.2	73.3	26.7	46.6
Lincolnshire	63.7	74.7	25.3	49.4
Merseyside	62.7	64.8	35.2	29.6
Norfolk	63.8	70.1	29.9	40.2
Northamptonshire	66.7	69.5	30.5	39.0
Northumberland	65.0	69.2	30.8	38.4
Nottinghamshire	63.1	66.8	33.2	33.6
Oxfordshire	67.7	73.6	26.4	47.2
Salop	62.0	72.3	27.7	44.6
Somerset	67.7	69.6	30.4	39.2
Staffordshire	64.3	67.4	32.6	34.8
Suffolk	64.9	72.2	27.8	44.4
Surrey	70.1	76.2	23.8	52.4
Sussex, East	65.8	74.3	25.7	48.6
Sussex, West	68.6	76.2	23.8	52.4
Tyne and Wear	62.7	62.9	37.1	25.8
Warwickshire	68.0	69.9	30.1	39.8
West Midlands	62.5	65.1	34.9	30.2
Wiltshire	67.8	71.7	28.3	43.4
Yorkshire, North	64.3	76.3	23.7	52.6
Yorkshire, South	62.4	63.4	36.6	26.8
Yorkshire, West	63.6	65.4	34.6	30.8
Welsh Counties				
Clwyd	65.8	69.1	30.9	38.2
Dyfed	67.5	67.6	32.4	35.2
Glamorgan, Mid	66.6	56.9	43.1	13.8
Glamorgan, South	66.7	69.5	30.5	39.0
Glamorgan, West	67.4	61.6	38.4	23.2
Gwent	68.2	62.1	37.9	24.2
Gwynedd	64.3	70.6	29.4	41.2
Powys	67.9	74.3	25.7	48.6
Scottish Regions				
Borders	63.2	72.3	27.7	44.6
Central Scotland	64.1	59.7	40.3	19.4
Dumfries and Galloway	61.5	68.2	31.8	36.4
Fife	63.3	56.3	43.7	12.6
Grampian	57.4	58.2	41.8	16.4

146

	Turnout	Yes	No	Yes Lead (in percentage points)
Highland	58.7	54.6	45.4	9.2
Lothian	63.6	59.5	40.5	19.0
Orkney	48.2	61.8	38.2	23.6
Shetland	47.1	43.7	56.3	−12.6
Strathclyde	61.7	57.7	42.3	15.4
Tayside	63.8	58.6	41.4	17.2
Western Isles	50.1	29.5	70.5	−41.0

Source: *The Times,* June 7, 1975. (The turnout figures were calculated after deducting the votes of servicemen, who voted where they were stationed and not where they were on the electoral register.)

INDEX

Cover and book design: Pat Taylor